A TIME FOR DREAMERS

To the people who have helped me during the years in order to produce this book and to all who are interested in the creative process ... the dreamers who have a vision of a better world and future for humanity.

Nilofar Mehrin

A TIME FOR DREAMERS

AUSTIN MACAULEY
PUBLISHERS LTD.

A CIP catalogue record for this title is available from the British Library.

ISBN 978 184963 292 8

www.austinmacauley.com

First Published (2013)
Austin Macauley Publishers Ltd.
25 Canada Square
Canary Wharf
London
E14 5LB

Printed and bound in Great Britain

Contents

Living Art As A Work in Progress

"The Poet"
mixed media collage, 1990

I was talking to a friend, who painted and was a teacher at an American university in Florence. He was a web designer and had done many websites for artists he knew. He had seen my studio and my cards[1] and said, "Why don't you write a story to go with your cards?" I had always wanted to write such a story, but I didn't think real life would allow me any flights of the imagination. That's why I thought about writing about the times I lived in.

I have always wondered about art meaning different things in different countries. As an example of recent successful

---

[1] The inshallah cards are reproductions of water colours and acrylic paintings. I sold these in shops from 1998-2013.

artists, I have been thinking about Tracy Emin and Damien Hirst's art, because they represent my generation. I want to talk about who I am by talking about their work, the ones that are important to me. Two pieces, the 'Unmade Bed' and the 'Camping Tent' are both on my list, and these two made me reflect on the personal dimension we associate with them. I identify with the human warmth and vulnerability of these.

Perhaps the ideal is the intimate heart feelings which are expressed in poetry and art, but one wonders if these have anything to do with the more materialistic dimension; is it the dichotomy between body and soul? I remember reading a quote from Heine, the German poet, where he said that he had pleasure looking at a person's face without wanting to possess them. However, he knew that he was an exception to the rule, and that generally people are interested in copulating and reproducing themselves, and some call that "love".

Personal feelings sometimes do express themselves in acts of copulation. It seems to me that from the 90s onwards, the "genital" has been the "only" interesting event in an individual's life. Inexplicably, people's sexuality has come out of prudish attitudes and has become a public domain. In society many are seen to be clutching, scratching , touching or indicating their private parts in a trendy, "must do" style.

On the other hand, there is another artist who I am interested in and who became successful in these decades. Damien Hirst is best known for his animal sections suspended in formaldehyde. His work made art and science seem one and the same thing. The cold scientific dimension is detached and formal. Awe inspiring nature was put in a show case, and humbled the spectator by putting him in his place as a mammal, which demonstrated that humans have the same machine parts inside of them as the other species. Being a religious minded person, I identify with these works of art and see them as a celebration of the hand of God; the supreme intelligence.

I first thought about writing when I read my grandfather's books. He was a historian, an expert in antiquity and Persia, and although he had had an adventurous life travelling the world over, his books were very difficult to read. I saw a lot of him when I was a child and he would talk about the things that had happened in his life. I always wondered why he didn't write about them, because those were the things which I was most interested in. I wanted to know about the feelings involved, the whys and the wherefores, rather than listen to his lessons in history.

Like Tracy Emin's 'Tent', in my writing and in my art[2] – however humble it may be – I want to say that I shared moments of my life with many people. Feelings for friends and relatives filled my days and my decisions. The times I lived in included a common history, shared with a lot of other individuals who were walking the earth at the same time as myself. As in the past centuries, when the world was not yet a "village", I would presume to think of Madame de Stael and other women writers who travelled and wrote about the times they lived in. Mine is not a testimony to the things which I have seen and felt – it is more a looking back on the events.

I would certainly not have bought a ticket to go to Italy if there hadn't been the Iran/Iraq[3] war in the 80s, or had I been born in my aunts' generation. Being Asian and from a Muslim family, I was born in Iran during the Shah's time, when women were wearing Western clothes. Even then, being a woman meant family ties and duties were utmost on the list of priorities. As role models, my father's sisters, my aunts Homa – who worked as a nurse – and Tahmeen – who was an office worker – had travelled to Europe after the Second World War, they were from a generation which was still oppressed by womanhood and the duties it entailed.

The older generation in my father's family had been brought up in India by their Iraqi mother who lived in Purdah,

---

[2] My view of sentiments expressed is certainly traditional and prudish but I realise Tracy Emin is expressing a general mood in her art which belongs to the Western experience.

[3] In my opinion The Iran/Iraq war in the beginning of the eighties made the arms trade very happy and also some nationalists who wrongly believed in establishing an age old belief in the Aryan racial superiority. It was tailor made in order to destroy both countries.

and later had moved to Iran. They had arrived in Tehran in the 1950s, and even though they worked, they were looking after their ailing father, and Parveen their sister, who perhaps suffered from autism, an ailment which had not been discovered yet.

With a lot of luck, I was born in times when I could afford to have time to myself for some years. Both my mother and her sister and their families were living in relative comfort, and as modern women. They managed to have a life which belonged to them, even if they had a family and were raising children. My mother had had a journalistic career and had written for the *Tehran English Daily* papers. She had an MA in English, having studied in India. She and my father had both been translators, and were intellectually alive. The younger generation too had had a university education; my cousins Ameneh and Sadieh who were born in Pakistan had degrees, and were women who were working. They were positive role models.

In Iranian society, having time to yourself for a woman was never considered to be a positive thing. That was the difference with my relatives in the subcontinent. The ideal Iranian woman had to be serving the children and everyone else in the family, and had to always be there for other people. Even now, 'most women' have no time to dwell on ideas and want to get on with their day-to-day lives, and they thrive as consumers. As a born Iranian, I was destined to be influenced by the history and culture of my country in the 60s, and the seventies during the reign of the Shah. One of the main productions of this time was a weekly periodical called *Ketabe Hafteh* ('The Book of the Week'), in which one could read translations of literary pieces from various countries and times. There were also articles about world art and culture.

Even though Iranians are very involved in their own literature, back then, the times were allowing many Western and Eastern ideas in. Like many other Asians, Iranians, both men and women, are brought up "trained" to have to shoulder much responsibility in the home, especially with the sick and the elderly. Even the middle classes work hard in the house, and are not like the middle classes elsewhere, who usually can afford to have help in the house and therefore have time to spend on their interests.

The home I was brought up in was totally strange according to the usual Iranian mentality, because at home the men, usually my father, cooked the meals. It would be unheard of for an Iranian husband to cook and prepare the meals, but my parents lived this way and my father would often tell me not to tell anyone about it, as he knew it would be an issue with everybody outside our home. My mother was a capable business woman. She was good at negotiating and pulling off deals. This was mostly because she was allowed to have self-confidence, and due to necessity she used her talents. Her sister, who had married a Pakistani and went to live in the UK, was very much the same type.

This was the background which made my case a special one, and I would describe my art to be a mixture of various cultures which have influenced me. I was born and bought up in Iran/Tehran, where I lived from 1959 to 1977. In 1978 I discovered London, staying with my mother's brother Ismile and his Swedish wife Ylva. Even as a child I spent some years in London with them. I went to the local primary and secondary schools along with my cousins. Some holidays were spent with my family in Karachi. These were different influences, and my family has given me a varied cultural background.

I have always been interested in expressing my own ideas. Even as a child, I would insist on not copying reality but saying something new which was on my mind. Sometimes I would produce bigger pieces, which were totally from my own imagination – I mean, not having copied from any source. This made one point of discord, with a lot of people who thought that copying reality was necessary.

One person at the foundation course[4] in London which I went to in 1980, who was a photographer, told me that the Persian miniatures themselves were the artworks of people

---

[4] Saint Martin's School of Art Foundation course

who had looked at reality closely and studied plants, objects, buildings and people in order to produce their own pictures. In other words, art was a language and one needed to know the words – i.e. arts and words were images from reality, and you had to learn them in order to then put them together to express an idea.

Fortunately, my own tutor Janet, who was a painter, was not hung up on such ideas. She said that she started to paint one day by simply putting all sorts of objects on the kitchen table and painting them because she had the urge to do it. I thought it a much more liberating and fun point of view. There was heart and emotion in the idea of doing things the way she did. It was a personal research, with her interest in life as the motivation and the engine. It meant that one could pick out the objects and things that one loved, put them on a table, and paint them. The important thing for her was that one should work, work, work, and the more you did this, the better. Working seriously for yourself was good, and if you were honest with yourself, you were going in the right direction.

In fact, Janet's pictures were so much of herself and very intimate. I thought it was kind of her to tell the young people who she taught that they should work hard at what interested them.

After the foundation course, I was going to study further, but then the times had changed, and even though I had a chance to study in an art polytechnic, I couldn't pay for it. This was because of the revolution in Iran and then the Iraq/Iran war, which had begun in 1981-82.

When the revolution broke out, I had gone to Pakistan to visit my parents. I had not been able to return to England because when I returned to attend my course in Cambridge, I was held at the airport and sent back with the excuse that in my diary I had expressed the wish to stay on in London, where I had already spent three years. It just happened that people like me, totally out of the reality of events in Tehran, were now victims of what Iranian "revolutionaries" – mostly have nots – decided to do back home. They had decided to get into the American Embassy grounds, which I thought seemed pretty unnecessary for them to do. I had to go back to my parents who were visiting family in Pakistan and Karachi. I spent and stayed a year in Karachi, living with my mother and her sister.

My Aunt Jahan's house in Karachi was very much a social hub, and was lots of fun and alive. My aunt and her daughter, my cousin Ameneh, were very socially active and great cooks. They would have lunches and dinners, and went to parties which made life lively and full of different interesting people. Through one of my aunt's friends there, I was introduced to an employment and worked at a graphic agency as an assistant. I was twenty one, and even though my parents wanted to see me settled down, my own dream was to get an education in Europe.

My mother had studied and was teaching English, and I thought that perhaps a degree in art wasn't really good enough for getting a practical paying job. She herself hadn't wanted me to go to an art school.

My parents had been born and brought up in India, in the Persian community which had lived there for several generations. They were brought up in Bangalore and Mysore, whereas my grandfather from my father's side had been born and brought up in Hyderabad by his Irani parents, and my mother's father had been a Shirazi, but had a history in Egypt and Iraq.

It seems that in their days, people could get on a horse or carriage and travel all over Asia without having to have specific papers[5]. I have this idea because of my grandfather's stories about how he had travelled from India to Iraq and back many times. He had actually started out from Hyderabad and worked on a ship taking tea to Japan when he was eighteen. From there, he had travelled to Europe and then to the United States. He then became a student in a university in the US, and lived there for a while. He even survived the earthquake in 1906 in California, and came back to Iraq to marry his first

_____

[5] Perhaps as President Putin suggested (I read in the papers) an Asian Union of countries, following the example of the European Union, could be our dream for a future peaceful Middle East and a source of prosperity for all Asian countries. Amen!

cousin, who was a girl brought up in Purdah and from a wealthy family. He took her and the children to India, where he was teaching Persian History and Literature at the University in Mysore.

Now, at twenty-two in Karachi, I had decided that I wanted to go back to Europe. My mother thought that I would get married to someone or the other in the family. She wasn't really in control and my father wasn't that interested in controlling my life. I had spent days in London where I was not sure about my future. I thought that I would have to change too much in order to be "a modern woman" if I integrated with the English way of life. It seemed to be too complicated, and I had always the idea that Italy was closer to my heart emotionally speaking. Even the language seemed to open doors of a different kind of modernity, as it were.

The summer of 1982, I was on a plane to Perugia and heading for the Universita per Straineri, where I stayed and studied Italian for three months. Then, since Florence seemed to be a smaller place than Rome – I couldn't handle living in a metropolis like London without family – and it was famous for art. I packed my bags again and went to a printing studio to see how etchings were made. I had seen these beautiful etchings in and around Russell Square where I went to school in London, and I wanted to make some myself, but the technique stood in my way of immediate expression.

In 1983, I got a job and started living with Dona, a girl who studied at an American university and was a photographer. I shared a flat with her in Via Maggio, and started working as a salesperson.

In 1984 I put my name down for a course at the university in order to study English Language and Literature. I didn't know Italian well enough, but I was living and learning.

Later in 1984, I had moved to Via Bolognese and was living with a group of young students. In 1985, I moved to Via delle Cinque Giornate with Peter, who was a German friend, then a PHD student, and his girlfriend Caterina.

I had gotten to know my fiancé Guido in Rome in 1983 and wanted to get married. My twenties were flying by and I was aspiring to art, as always, but not getting much done, since I had to make a living as a salesperson.

From 1984 to 1989, I was beginning to paint big pictures in Via delle Cinque Giornate. Peter had gone back to Germany and now I sub-rented the rooms to other students and worked as a salesperson in the summer. The apartments I had lived in had always meant so much to me, and in this last one I lived for fifteen years, renting out the extra rooms to other students.

At university I was getting along, slowly learning the Italian language. It was very hard. Guido had been a great help after I failed to get through the first exam at university. He made it a point to help me get through the first exams. He had become my personal trainer, but I found it very hard to study, because when I studied books, I would want to paint as well, and I was very much distracted by the different directions that these two interests took me. On one hand, I had to have a fixed timetable in order to study, and on the other hand, I needed to get the ideas out on paper or canvas and give them a structure.

My cousin Ameneh, who was a journalist and working for a newspaper, came to visit me from Pakistan and asked, "why didn't you continue going to an art School and study art?" Why was I studying literature when I loved to make pictures? The answer was that I was not confident of being an artist, but I had these ideas that would push me to spend money on canvas and paint. I would collect a lot of art material for the times when I had the moments of high energy, and I would paint when I was emotionally stressed out. It was a sort of discipline. I even refused to get angry and fight for a relationship, and I would take my energies to the canvas.

It seemed that the people I had in my life never listened to me. I mean, I hadn't a voice and I found that was a problem in almost every sphere of my life. I suppose women only find a voice and people listen to them only if they have a tough man on their side like my mother had, or if they have children or a tough personality. I kept on asking the men in my life to get married and they would only come round to doing it after several years had passed.

My mother had had a strong voice of authority because she was a first child, and being very bright, everyone gave her a lot of attention. Even Ameneh was like her. Everyone listened to them. I hadn't managed to learn to have a similar voice. Perhaps I wasn't a fighter, and she was more aggressive and competitive. I was most of the time struggling with myself, trying to get myself under control. I think that it had something to do with being very physical. I mean, I felt that I had an athletic constitution.

I was really vigorous, and yet I wanted to have a brain and to be an intellectual like my parents. I hated being in a woman's body. A female, whose God given role in life was to reproduce. I thought it was really humiliating to be a woman because women always seemed to be second class, like myself. They never achieved a voice until they had children, but I wanted to have respect effortlessly. I wanted people to listen to what I had to say, but they didn't.

I suppose it's normal to ask for things and not get them when you want them. I have come to think that the world is pretty much like that – unless you are lucky or you put a gun to people's head, you get to be second class. Even when I had been living in England and I asked my cousin if he wanted to get married, he said he wasn't ready because he was a student. I thought, I wish I could save him from being so far from his own culture. I wanted to save myself too. I thought that he was missing out on his Iranian and Pakistani cultural roots, but he didn't see it that way and, of course, I was wrong in my traditional mentality. It was like a story from a Jane Austen novel. Later on in life I saw the film 'West is West'[6] and it made me realise the emotional distances and the work that has to be done before it would have all worked out according to how I saw things.

I was stupid enough to ask him if he wanted to get married

---

[6] The British comedy directed by Andy De Emmony, 2010 is a film about a Pakistani who has two families, one in Punjab and one in Britain. This film is about the cultural misunderstandings and the solutions which eventually evolve out of the interactions between the people involved. It is very much relevant to my own background.

and later on, my aunt – his mother – told me that women are not supposed to ask and that they are supposed to wait until they are asked. And much later, about thirty years later, she told me that he had had many Indian and Pakistani families who were after him for their daughters.

I was only a woman who wanted to express all the things I couldn't handle like other women: like Emin's bed and tent, I was finding my way through relationships and I also needed to be an artist rather than want to get a marriage. Practical visa and stay permit concerns plus my own traditional upbringing made me have to propose to people myself! As an educated and modern woman, my mother's solution was surprising; she suggested that I could throw myself at the feet of one of her rich relatives and plead to him to marry me because all I really owned was my virginity.

I still think it couldn't have been her saying such a thing to her twenty-one year old daughter. She was probably worried about what people would say!

However, later on when I met Guido in Italy, I was crying for ages about what had happened to me and the humiliation that I had put myself through by asking my cousin that stupid question. And that is why in Islam, parents have to take responsibility to marry off their children. No one can twist your arm and make you do the right thing – most of the time, one has to make decisions oneself. It is the negotiation part that I find so difficult. My mother and my aunt were both good at negotiating, whereas I've always been totally at loss for words.

Guido was the eldest son of a lawyer, and he was very articulate. He would want to talk relentlessly at times. Once I had learnt the language, we would get into these conversations which were very funny and exhilarating, and that is when I realised that it is the spiritual thing of wanting to communicate. I never dreamed of meeting a man who would want to talk to me! But I suppose most men, even the ones that want to talk, usually have difficulty in listening to women.

Which brings me back to the subject of art and expression. I suppose art for me was all those things that I wanted to say, and I was making an effort to make myself listened to. But I think the first thing that I would tell people is that if you use art as a message to mankind, then use it wisely. I know that if you are a black person or a woman or gay, you have always been at a disadvantage because, only the man with "the gun" or "the power of words" has been able to put his foot down and has had the last word. It seems that is what this world is all about. But art too is a powerful instrument. I read an interview with the German film director Fassbinder some years ago. In this, he stated that even though he was from the same angry generation as the Bader-Meinhoff and he knew them, he had chosen a different path in order to express his opinions through the films he made. I thought that was very intelligent.

Most of my life I've seen that only "power" has a voice. Perhaps having a voice, is powerful too. You can say something and be heard in art. That's the beauty of the thing. And your message has to be a good one...

I started to make the Inshallah cards in 1989 and1990. Then, in 1992, I managed to get my degree in English Language and Literature from Florence University. I was having shows and exhibits in and around Florence. I loved to go to Venice and the carnival there, and later on I did some watercolours on Venice, which is a beautiful city and a constant source of inspiration.

In 1998, I had to leave the apartment[7] where I had lived for fifteen years. With help from friends and well-wishers I managed to get a studio in the centre of Florence, and I started to sell my watercolours to the public. My watercolours were about the city were I had lived for the past twenty years, and the sitting rooms and interiors I painted were a dream of finding a stable home.

I was trying to live on my art, producing a lot of watercolours, cards and boxes. My clients were mostly tourists. I lived in the same place upstairs. My studio was in a back street in the centre and I was living like a hermit with lots

---

[7] The via delle cinque giornate street (which translates to The Five days of Milan), was the apartment belonging to Mr. Quercioli, which me and my friends rented in 1984, it is where I lived for 15 years.

of cats, who I loved. I couldn't make money and pay the rent after 2001, but I paid my assistants to come and help me produce in quantity. I really had no business sense at all, so in a frustrating way I helped a competitor who had been watching me to take over my sphere of sales, i.e. the shop I was selling in. This person who does admirable etchings became very successful in selling his art because, out of feelings of solidarity with artists, I had shared my own distributor with him. Finding that his machine produced work took over my hand made one and out of naivety I lost a very important source of income.

In 2001 shops closed down and I had to leave the studio. In 2004, I spent some time in Viareggio and in 2005 in the spring, I went back to Iran, to my mother, who was suffering from Alzheimer's. I decided to buy property in Dubai, and in 2007 I rented a house in Dubai for one year. I continued to paint in Tehran, and had the help of young students and assistants who worked for me in my home studio.

My story is far from a success story – if anything I am probably the anti-heroine in the novel who did everything wrong. However, I think it is a story which shows a generation who aspired to create a new voice; one which is neither Eastern nor Western, but in the middle of the crossroads. According to President Angela Merkel, the multicultural society hasn't worked out in Germany – and probably she meant Europe – but people like me believe that it is a new project and it has to be given time. The painting 'Existence' or 'The Contact' is about reaching out to get to know the other.

Perhaps in Asia, where many different tribes live together, you can see this voice; it is there in many Indian and Pakistani films. The Middle East is something different and more complex. Israel and its creation marks all the Muslims; it is a nation born out of European mistakes, and brings suffering to the rest of the Middle Eastern people. Will it ever be able to integrate – i.e. make friends with – its neighbours, or will it take over all of the Middle East through Zionistic pressure groups? My painting 'Energies and Tendencies' is talking about a mutation in geographical terms.

In 2008, I fell victim to anonymous security people who didn't allow me to buy property and move to Dubai. All through the new century, the new world order has wanted to take our voice away from us. This sense of being made into "puppets on a string" is in the painting 'J'aillais me donner'.

I associate my science fiction planetary paintings with the more detached and scientific part of my imagination. Planetary science can be a refuge from our imperfect lives on earth. We have to live in the shelter of our buildings and sitting rooms and bedrooms, and even though there are now six billion of us on the planet, our emotional lives hinder us from finding solutions to problems. Today we are worried about resources.

While spirituality teaches us that resources are infinite if we aspire to higher values, the materialistic view limits our potential to find new solutions. It is the difference between Chairman Mao and Churchill's way of dealing with the food problem. While the latter called for an increase in positive individual participation to cultivate and grow food, the former took for granted that some were going to be victims of the famine anyway. Just as today, some believe that nature is bound to get destroyed anyway. Here I would like to mention and pay tribute to the millions of people – some say 45, but I imagine the number to be higher – who died in the famine during the recent years in China, due to a lack of interest and energy in trying to save them. The melting down of the glaciers will happen, polar bears and other animals will die of starvation and climate change will inevitably change our planet and our life for the worse.

One aspires towards higher things, but will we ever manage to pull ourselves up and do the right thing? None of us is finding a solution to the problems, and the reason is that we lack the imagination to find and implement new ideas to the vital issues which are decisive for the future of the planet. Meanwhile, we will be scratching our genitals, and hiding our heads in the sand, being totally irresponsible and decadent. Like puppets on a string, we leave our destiny to God, and to the powers that be.

Staying with my Uncle and Aunt in London

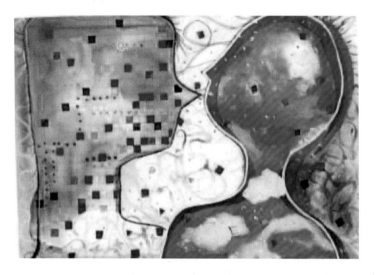

Dialogue
Watercolour, 1988

My Uncle Ismile had been living in the UK in London ever since he was eighteen, until he died in 1999 or thereabouts when he was sixty-three. He was born in Bangalore like my mother, but he considered himself a Pakistani rather than Persian.

He was important in my life because I stayed with him and his wife Ylva for three years when I went to study in England in 1979. I was just out of high school, having taken my last exam for my diploma. Having finished high school at eighteen,

I looked forward to going to England and staying with them in London.

My mother was his elder sister of about 10 years, and as her family had accepted to keep me at school in London with them even when I had been a child. Now she asked him to help her get me into university in Britain. I was always a very dull, uniformed young thing with no one to guide me. I was more than happy to escape the university entrance exams in Tehran as they seemed a barrier which seemed impossible for me to overcome.

**The Persian carpet
Oil on canvas, 2008**

I had been an absolutely useless student, mediocre by all definitions at high school. The only subject that I was good at was English because as a child, I had been sent to stay with my Auntie Jahan and her three children. My Uncle Ismile and his wife Ylva lived together with my Auntie Jahan in the southeast of London, in a semi-detached house. Later they moved to a house which they renovated themselves. They were very different from us Iranians as they did a lot of DIY and enjoyed it.

The highlight of my high school in Iran, was when I once did a synopsis of the book *1984*, introducing George Orwell to my seventeen year old class mates. I suppose I am still happy about that, because a lot of other students were proud of their maths and science exams, and I usually never excelled in anything. However, having gone to primary school in the UK as a kid, my English was pretty good and then it is true, that my mother, God bless her soul, tried to get me interested in the subject of books and novels by telling me the stories of these, and that is how I was introduced to the stories of Shakespeare and other authors.

She was an English Literature MA from Bangalore University and she loved books herself. Her efforts – whatever little effort she put in teaching me – were fruitful and even later on in life, I followed her on that path, being too afraid of risking a useless degree in art. That is what my Mother thought because we were ignorant of the fact that art was an important subject. Here I want to tell everybody that a degree in art can be as useful as any other. My Uncle Ismile had heard his fair share of stories too, because he was my mother's youngest brother and she tried to get him to study with the same methods.

The sitting room looking on to the river Arno
Watercolour, 2007

I had always been a plain girl, whereas my Pakistani cousins Ameneh and Atefeh, with whom I stayed with in London, were much more interesting and brilliant girls. Everyone was always talking about them. What they did and said, was of the utmost importance. They were special perhaps because their father had died and also because Auntie Jahan and her Brother and his wife genuinely liked to communicate with children and judged them to be above average.

My aunt and uncle and Ylva, my uncle's Swedish wife, thought the world of Ameneh, the eldest child. She was truly the star on top of the Christmas tree. People would have thought that she was some sort of a genius in the making. My uncle, they say, was pretty much obsessed with her when she had been a teenager, and he hadn't allowed my aunt to bring up her children in the Islamic Pakistani tradition. The girls had pretty much a British type of education and upbringing.

In 1979, when I arrived at their home with my mother when I was eighteen, my cousins weren't living there. Ameneh was at Brighton University studying science, and Farid was at Swansea. Sadly, Atefeh had passed away in Pak/Karachi at the age of sixteen from an unidentified illness. She had fallen into a coma and died. Atefeh had gone to Karachi to live with her mother and go to school there.

Atefeh had been my childhood friend. We were very different; she was seemingly shy and retiring and looked very feminine, and liked all the girly things. She loved to dress up and to look pretty, she liked to write and had lots of friends. When in Karachi we would all go to the bazaar in the old part of town to buy glass bangles and nice materials to give to the tailor. It was very exciting to be with my cousins because they knew so many people and were always involved. We visited jewellery stores with our mothers. We weren't really that interested in the gold ourselves, but the older generation bought it with the idea that gold would always come in handy one day.

Once I was invited with her to a school friend's house and we went to this party where all the girls and boys were sixteen like us, and we had to stay the night because it got very late. I woke up early with the call for prayer and even though I didn't pray regularly, I felt I had to pray. I couldn't think of something to cover up with so I used a bed sheet, putting it over my head and as I was praying. Naturally someone in the house woke up to go to the loo and in the dark they saw this sheet moving on its own. There was a low frightened scream because they thought I was a ghost.

That happened some months before Atefeh went into a coma. It was probably some kind of sign. We had had such good times together when some months earlier she and her family had come to Tehran. They had driven from London, travelling across Eastern Europe and Turkey all the way in an old green Peugeot. My aunt had bought it second hand in London.

It was the summer of 1976, and when they arrived at our old house, everything seemed just perfect...

Just some months before she passed away, we had spent some memorable evenings on the rooftop of my old house in Tehran. In those years, people still slept in the open air, on the rooftops in the summer. The beds would be laid out in the cool evenings and by nighttime they were deliciously cool and fresh to sleep in. We were both sixteen and slept close to each other. We watched the stars and talked and giggled until we fell asleep. Even then we had noticed the red planet and we didn't know it was the planet Mars, which would soon descend upon the country.

The night of the Angels
Oil on canvas, 1988

Uncle Ismile and Auntie Ylva were a nice middle aged couple,
who were dreaming of their pension years when I went to stay
with them. It was because of Ylva's Swedish influence that
they lived a very methodic and organised kind of life. Ylva
was generous enough to see her husband go back to university
at forty.

Al Noor
Oil on canvas, 1987

He got his degree in economics and was then able to teach at high school. They were both teachers, going to work every day. They would come home, cook the evening meal and we would eat together at the table, where my uncle talked politics and me and my aunt kept quiet, only because we didn't really care one way or the other.

I had been enrolled in a crash course, studying three A-levels in order to pass them in one year. No one told me that it was an impossible task for someone who wasn't a real studying maniac.

However, I plodded along to Great Russell Street every day to the University Tutorial College and would spend the lunch hour at the British Museum. Of course I didn't get through the exams as I should have.

My Time
Mixed media, 1989

Whereas the Iranian students and the other Indian and Pakistani students who had taken languages or Maths for their subjects passed and were accepted into university by the end of two years study, I only managed to get a pass for English and Biology in my A levels, and I had spent a lot of time painting.

I am grateful to my uncle for allowing me to try going to art school. It was my own choice, and that's what I really wanted to do in the first place but hadn't had the courage in that direction. So I came home to my uncle one day and said I had enrolled at Saint Martin's on a foundation course and I was going to try to get a degree in art.

I suppose people knew that I liked drawing and painting, as I had always done those things when I should have been studying for my exams. That year at Saint Martin's was a good year. I had finally found my place and was happy to go on studying art.

Going to Italy was the result of my wanting to study and to get a degree. I hadn't managed to do it in England. Mrs Thatcher and the Conservative Government in 1981 brought about the rise in costs to attend university, and the revolution in Iran meant that I didn't have the money.

The last time I met my uncle and aunt in Florence, they were both older, in their sixties and enjoying their pensions. Now they had all the time in the world to travel in Europe as they had always wanted to do. The first thing that we did when they got off the train that came from Milan airport, La Malpensa, was naturally to go to a coffee shop and get a cappuccino.

My Uncle still had a lot of his thick white hair, with the exception of a bald patch that he was getting at the back of his head. Auntie Ylva was looking very old and tired.

Joseph's Dream
Oil on canvas, 1988

Not working hadn't made their life more pleasant for them. I had always been very grateful to them both for their support and friendship, and so I was sad to see them unhappy even as pensioners.

My aunt wore a hard expression because of the problems that she had had to face in her life. Now my uncle wasn't well, and she had to look after him and nurse him. He also had a girlfriend that he had introduced to the family; it was none of my business in the first place, but his choice rocked my conservative view of life. It hadn't happened in our family that anyone should take a 2nd wife, but I know it happens all the time… I mean divorces and other relationships happen all the time and are in the normal way of life for everyone. There was something wrong or right with families who remained the same all through. My parents pulled through fifty years of marriage and were an exception to the rule.

This 'other woman' happened to be an eighteen year old, one of his students and from East Germany. This story reminded me of a film called *Icelandic Wedding*, where a young girl marries the teacher and accepts the fact that each one has a life of their own. She does not expect too much of the institution called marriage. Whereas the 1st wife chooses to die because she finds that he is never there for her and that she has lost him somewhere along the years.

My grandmother as a child (Saheb Soltan) and her sister

These two people were now sitting in front of me in the coffee shop in the Piazza della Stazione. I could feel that they were really lonely and lost, and as if they were both in need of an adult person to look after them.

My uncle had always been a sort of leftist-secular liberal who didn't believe in religion and he never talked about God. In fact, God didn't come into his vocabulary at all.

Whereas his father, Mr Namazie, who was a Shirazi, was a very religious minded Shia, and he was brought up in the Holy city of Kazemain. He used to spend most of his time praying and reading the Holy Koran, and not much time at his business making money in Bangalore where he lived with his wife Mrs Saheb-Soltan Shustari, daughter of a Mullah. Their three sons had all taken a dislike to religion and wanted to be modern and practical, and they were secular.

My uncle, being the youngest of the five children, was very down to earth and wanted to get things done. Getting organised and living in the world's reality meant everything to him. All he talked about were political subjects. One of his favorite topics at the dinner table was what the German Nazis did during the war in Europe. He would repeat that the Holocaust of the Jewish people included, aside from the six million Jews, other people as well. He would go on and on, saying that we all must be responsible people, doing our bit for society, contributing to society and so forth.

I learnt a lot of Communist jargon from his dinner time monologues. He wasn't Islamic at all; only once did he mention God, and that was when one summer I was going out a lot without telling him where I was going. I only went to museums in London, but once I ventured out to France, to Paris, to see a high school friend who was staying there. That time he said that God had created the planets according to a plan so that they went round their orbits with regular precision, and that's why the worlds that God had created were all interconnected and worked according to these precise and reliable movements, which were eternal and relied upon each other, moving in orbits destined by him. As in Sureh Al Rahman no 5.

Pulsar
Watercolour, 1990

His wife Ylva humoured his political sermons. Nobody, excepting Aunt Jahan and myself and her daughter Ameneh, remembers what he said in his repetitions of the same concepts. My aunt remembered them because she was mischievously making fun of him when he wasn't around. It was such a relief to see that someone didn't take him seriously!

Auntie Ylva and myself, who were intimidated by him, used to listen patiently at lunch and dinner. His voice of male authority didn't encourage anyone else to get a word in. Sometimes my aunt use to try and get a bourgeois table discussion off the ground. She would say, "wasn't it true that this happened in history?" Just something to liven up the monologue. When she did speak, she highlighted his words by her wavering and indecisive manner. He was the one in charge, and his words were somehow unique and nothing could be said to match their importance.

I used to wonder at him, since my father and brother never tried to prove anything to anyone. In fact, nobody I knew was so self-absorbed as he was. Especially his standing up for the Jewish people in our Palestinian suffering region.

The Germans had always been morally beaten down after the Second World War. They were portrayed as terrible humans; people who heartlessly helped the Fuhrer to be the dictator that he was. Hollywood and all English productions on the subject of the war have always been full of propaganda which we all know well. However, in Iran and the Arab countries, Germans had always been looked up to because they were known to be so efficient, unlike ourselves, they were disciplined, capable and neutral.

For other reasons we liked the Germans and thought that they were more tolerant towards us in the Middle East than most of the 'white men' and their civilisations. They were involved in other issues with other nations, and that was reassuring for a lot of people. Being reliable, clear minded and straightforward and sincere and not very friendly, made these people seem more acceptable.

The Israeli war on the Palestinians, the plight of the Arabs and their homelessness, was what he should have been talking about and what he did say about the subject was unrealistic. He said that if all the Arabs got united, there wouldn't be room for "the state of apartheid" in the Middle East. But we all knew that this was not a solution and that it would never happen. The future would probably allow the state of Israel to survive and flourish – the injustice to the Palestinians was obvious and inevitable and nobody could do anything about it. Only a miracle could save the Palestinians and the Middle East from this, and a miracle was nowhere in sight.

The Blue Apartment in 1997

Having said that, accepting this reality also made people in the Middle East look at Israel as a creation of Europeans who had always been intolerant and had kept the hatred against the Jewish nation fueled for centuries. The Muslims had to pay the price for European crimes and history. Whilst the Western countries had created their oasis in the dessert, Israel was now their 'darling' and everything that nation did was right and good.

I traveled to Iran in the early 1990s, when I was thirty-two. My best friends in Florence were Sharon who was American, and Sara who was Australian. Sharon was Jewish from her mother's side, but she denied being Jewish because she said that her father was a Christian white American. She was blondish and blue eyed, and no one could actually tell from her appearance that she was a New York Jewess and possibly a Zionist.

I liked her, even though my heart told me that she was probably not on my side. I was grateful for her leftist political conversations because she was informed. Ordinary people in Europe were really not that interested in world politics, unless they were students or intellectual of some kind. Those were the 1980s and 1990s, when 9/11 hadn't been 'created' to brainwash the world.

That summer, I had been painting my apartment blue.

'Da Sein'
(which translates to 'Being There' from Heidegger
Acrylic on canvas, 1991

During the spring of 1992, I had had a court case against the shop where I use to work for some years, during the summer months. My lawyer was a young, handsome Florentine.

The picture below was a homage to those white people in the corridors of power, who have controlled the world events after World War Two with the utmost nonchalance. 'Entente Cordial' is the name.

'Entente cordial, (or Goodbye to Palestine)'
Watercolour, 1988

Sharon would say things which I had heard my uncle say, the same leftist arguments. It was so reassuring! I was happy to be friends with her because she was intellectually alive and sensitive, where other people really couldn't be bothered. For example, she was interested in the Bosnian War, and she was moved by the events happening in central Eastern Europe as much as I was.

It was now 1994 and my uncle hadn't liked me staying on in Florence after getting my degree in 1992. I suppose he thought that I should have left Italy, and that my staying on in Europe after my BA was really unnecessary. After they arrived at the train station, I had taken them back to my apartment.

When they came to the house, I was showing Auntie Ylva my paintings; she had bought some paintings from me in the past. I had done this huge one of the sea-barrier reef. It was two or three metres big and it was a lovely peaceful picture. I called it 'Underwater Scene'. Of course I showed it to her with an interest in selling it, as I was penniless and I don't deny that slimy money intention underneath the exposure of my work.

'Panorama Subacquea' or 'Underwater Scene'
Oil on canvas, 1989

She did admire the picture, and I was happy to show it to someone who appreciated it. Little did I know that my uncle was seething! I suppose it was as if he had been a child who had lost his mother's attention for one minute, and he didn't like me having done something which wasn't under his control. I can imagine the reason and the psychology that lay behind his anger. He started to say some very unpleasant things then, and I just stood there and took those words silently, thinking, oh my God! Why do I deserve this being shouted at and called names? Later on, when he'd cooled down, he confessed that he had always wanted to be an artist himself but couldn't afford to approach art.

He had to earn his living and had had to concentrate on the practicalities and other paths.

However, he didn't say he was sorry. I had learnt in another similar experience to take what was dished out from the elders with some philosophy, so we made an appointment for the next day, as if nothing had happened. Just as if no offensive words had been spoken. I suppose I only tolerated that scene because I was helpless and poor. Plus, I didn't want to fight with him in front of his wife. Later on, my brother said, "beggars can't be choosers" and that was me being a beggar. He was right in saying that I had received too much from my uncle. It is true that my uncle had been a real friend and had always helped me during the years at university. He had been a rock.

They stayed for a few days in a hotel in Via Nazionale because my uncle refused to stay in the blue apartment. I took them to Viareggio for the day. We went to a place right by the seaside and had lunch. Ylva and I were quiet, very subdued and a heavy air of dark unresolved feelings was around us and in my heart. I was glad to see them go back to the UK.

My uncle did give me some money as an atonement for his misbehavior and kind words before we parted, and I was grateful for that. He had always helped me out.

Some years later, I was left some money by my Aunt Ylva in her spoken will. She had suffered a stomach ailment and had come through the critical period, only to get a hospital infection. On her deathbed, she remembered me and asked her husband to give me £8,000. My Uncle was good enough to send me £3,000 of this sum, and I managed to go to Paris after years of hardship. The astonishing thing was that he had asked me to buy a small apartment for myself with this money! Then, when I told him that I had been to Paris, he didn't like that at all and was angry again.

He said that he would send me the rest of the inheritance left by my aunt, his wife, if I obeyed his one wish – i.e. he wanted me to promise that I would give up my ambition of becoming a painter.

I couldn't give up painting and art like he'd asked me to, since I was in the studio in Via Fiesolana since 1998 and had worked so much towards that goal. I told him that I wouldn't promise anything of the sort. It was ridiculous of him to ask me such a thing and he was going against all his leftist ideas.

He decided to keep the money, since he said that he had spent about £5,000 on me when I stayed with him in England.

It was very out of character. He wasn't the man he used to be some years ago and by saying such things, I was very confused about what I should do. His coming between me and my life's ambition seemed a bit too much, but I felt that it wasn't really him who was doing this. It was probably grief, as other out of character things did happen after Auntie Ylva passed away.

My uncle, who had never talked about any dark event in his childhood, started to say that the servants at home in India – he was a child of Bangalore – had mistreated him. It was totally unbelievable, especially since he hadn't given the minimum sign of such events all through the years in which we knew him. It was very embarrassing for us to hear him speak of such things now. However, now I understand that it was the psychological breakdown that was upon us and through this suffering, other venues – 'the dark forces' – had come to create mischief in our family relationships. Relationships which had been very peaceful until then.

His last year was spent in isolation, with his girlfriend who got married to him; who became his partner and looked after him. He was separated mentally from his loved ones, and none of us could do anything to make it better for him. He was lucky in that he could rely on his beloved second wife – ironically, she was German.

As usual, I was penniless all the while and couldn't even go to the UK to make up with him. Even when my Irish friend Michaela offered to go to his house and talk to him for my sake, as an ambassador of peace, I didn't accept it. I really didn't know how to interpret his behaviour; perhaps I should have accepted her offer, but then I didn't think that he would die in such a short time.

I am grateful to him, because he didn't hinder me to go to the art school that year in 1981.

Life is funny because we think that we have so much time ahead of us – but then we really don't. Every decision we make could be the most important one. 1981 was the year of the Iranian revolution, and from being well off, we were about to become very poor and discriminated against. Like many others of my countrymen, I had had a proposal from the Foreign Office visa section; if I didn't leave the country for three years, I would be given a British passport.

Even though this was a huge opportunity, I couldn't accept it because I felt that I was too confused in England and that I needed my family. So I left London to go to Karachi that summer and then regretted that decision very much. However, it was the best decision, the healthiest one and I feel good to have taken that step, even though it was hard for me later.

Studying and working in Florence, Italy, 1984 – 2005

I was twenty-four when I moved from Via Maggio to the students apartment in Via Bolognese. I had been living and working in the centre of Florence for nearly a year now. I had a job in the leather store in Borgo Santissima Apostali, right next to the fascinating old bridge the Ponte Vecchio. I had left the apartment in Via Maggio, where I had lived with Dona. This was in 1984, when Italy won the World Cup, and everyone went celebrating and didn't allow any peace and quiet until late.

Via Bolognese

I had left the Via Maggio apartment in 1984 because of the noise which only stopped from 3am to 5am in the morning. Later on, it became a traffic-controlled area, but I was happy to leave it for Via Bolognese. I loved the apartment in Via Bolognese because it was close to the countryside. Linda, who was English but married to an Italian, moved into the apartment in Via Maggio. She was younger than I was and later on got together with Daniele, the owner of the jewellery store I was working in. She seemed to follow me in my life.

Via Bolognese was an upper middle class sort of area; very quiet and conservative. In the apartment there were mostly people in their twenties, and they tended to be the student types. Peter had rented it, having found the place through his university where he was a PHD student. This, plus the fact that he was German, were good enough credentials for the landlord.

View from the bridge
Pencil on Paper, 1982

It wasn't the apartment itself but the views, the sights and sounds offered from the windows. You could see olive groves and fields from the windows. While other houses were far away, you heard the birds and the breeze in the trees rather than the noise of human activity. It was totally different from Via Maggio. We didn't bother much about the neighbours because we hardly ever saw them, except for the people who lived downstairs, for they were often in their garden.

It was a very big change from Via Maggio, which was a decadent type of deluxe apartment with parquet flooring and special lights. However, it did have some positive points. It was well furnished and central. It was very good for going to work in the centre. I used to walk to work in order to get a feel for the city as I went past cafes and the shops in the mornings. The buzz of the city, especially in the mornings, was very exciting.

People shouting friendly buongiornos to each other as their working day began. You felt the freshness of the new day. Then there was the Ponte, my favourite place to cross and go over to reach the commercial side of the town. I went along Via Gucciardini, looking at the shop windows before going on to the bridge, and then on to the Por Santa Maria.

Via Maggio area
Watercolour, 1999

The centre around Borgo SS. Apostoli was a little claustrophobic; a closed in sort of life. One didn't get away from the work routine and reality at all. Whereas, in Via Bolognese, you felt that you could finally hear yourself think. I was very grateful for the peace. The tranquillity of the place was true luxury.

In Via Maggio I had entertained people who I got to know through my flatmate Dona.

Her friend Sally was working in the same Por Santa Maria Road, in a shop selling textiles and materials. I had become friends with her even though we didn't have anything in common.

Borgo SS Apostoli
Watercolour, 2003

She was of a wealthy Californian family and had come to Florence for a holiday. Then she had decided to stay. She met a man who was working in the central market. A family man – Emilio. He was a tall man with orange coloured hair and lots of freckles.

We used to go out together at times and invite them over. They were a little older than I was. She was thirty two years old and wanted very much to get married to her boyfriend. However, when she did get married, she was bored out of her mind, living in the suburbs of Montecatini, without working or having much money to spend.

"The Thing In The Jar"
(An idea from a science fiction book)
Watercolour, 1983

Sally had married Emilio because she was getting on. She was already thirty two years old and by the time they got married and when she had a child, she was in her mid-thirties. She had probably got married for social reasons, because marriage is still a respectable thing to do and people accept that all over the world.

It didn't surprise me when later on she left Italy, going to visit her parents that Christmas. She was asking for a divorce when she got to the States. She had taken their daughter with her.

Her husband, who was very much a family man, felt depressed about her flight and especially about her having taken their child. Perhaps it was for the best. They went to the States because Sally realised the standard of living that she had to settle down to in Italy was much lower than what she was used to. Her husband was crying over the daughter being taken to California by Sally.

He followed them to the States to see if he could convince her to return and live with him once again. So much for money not being able to buy happiness! Sally probably did the right thing. For some people, it was such a dream to be able to go to the States, to learn a new language and try to live in Los Angeles. I couldn't understand anyone who didn't want a better life.

The Metropolis
Watercolour Collage, 2008

Gabriele, Dona's boyfriend from Florence, was smart, I thought because he had managed to get married and go to live with Dona in New York. But it took him quite a few years to do it.

Emilio was told by the American judge to keep away from his wife and child if he didn't wish to live in the United States. And so he was packed off to Italy to live his bachelor type of lifestyle all over again. But this time around, he chose to hang around with Filipino girls, who were flexible and cheerful.

Gabriele and Dona had met in a bar on the Lungarno. Dona was a young American student, studying with a program at Stanford University. I had met her through an American girl who was at the print school at Santa Reparata.

The Kitchen
Watercolour, 2004

I was telling someone that I lived at the campsite because I couldn't find an apartment. This kind girl knew Dona was looking for a flatmate, so she introduced me to her. Dona wasn't bothered that I was Iranian and Muslim, and I was happy that we could have a respectful relationship.

One day, she met Gabriele, who didn't speak English, and her Italian was pretty basic. Since working, I was speaking Italian quite well by now.

They were getting along quite well, even though they couldn't understand each other very well. Gabriele would make pasta tricolore for us.

Cosmopolitan Time, 1990
Oil on canvas

Then one day, Gabriele was banging on the door downstairs on the street and Dona wasn't opening it. He was banging and shouting and I was wondering what had happened... It was getting embarrassing. She sent me downstairs to talk to him and tell him to go away. Later on, we found out that it had been a cultural misunderstanding.

Gabriele was really very nice and gentle. He had been banging on the door vehemently because he wanted to explain things which he had said and done.

I was to translate, since I could understand both sides. I found that Dona was much more structured and law abiding, while Gabriele was a heart person, moved by his emotions. It took him quite a few years to persuade her that they could be good together.

"The Cathedral And My Friends"
1999

He went to the States several times, and Dona came to Florence several times, and they eventually became a family in the late 1980s. Dona had done some wonderful photographs of the Venice carnival in the early 1980s when we lived together, and later on she came to visit me when I had moved to Via delle Cinque Giornate.

Our life in the heart of the city was really mingling with other people. The apartment next door was very close. It had been one large apartment and now very elegantly separated with the installation of two separate entrance doors. I got to know William and Antonio, the two men living next door, through Dona's friendship with them.

Dona, who had introduced me to Sally, was a twenty three

year old photographer from New York. She had also been a ballet dancer, but told me that due to a mistake she had made, she had hurt her knee and had lost the opportunity of becoming a professional dancer.

William was English, and very charming in manner and looks. He also had a posh accent. We didn't know what he did for a living, and he didn't seem to do much.

It was absurd to think that he was supporting Antonio who was a simple Neapolitan young man, but Antonio went to an expensive art school in town. I used to envy Antonio so much for his going to that art school, as it was something I could only dream of doing.

The Old City
Watercolour, 2003

Dona, my flatmate, was fond of William, and they were the closest of friends. She got angry with me when I once suggested that the two men might be married to each other. One heard of all sorts of relationships other than the strictly orthodox ones. That was new for my sheltered mind and I didn't much like getting involved. I suppose I wished I had had a friend like Antonio seemed to have – he had found a true heart; a friend who believed in his art, and he was doing something that I hadn't the guts and the courage to invest in at the time.

I had gone to Italy with art being my priority, but I had come to lose all confidence in myself by having to earn a living and having to settle for a life of drudgery as a saleswoman – a life I wasn't happy with at all.

The Musician
Watercolour, 2002

My own fiancé, called Guido, was being difficult and didn't want to settle down. He said he wanted to buy a house or apartment first. He was following me to Via Bolognese and I didn't want him around and I told him so, but I couldn't do anything about him persisting to come along.

The Via Bolognese Apartment

I found Peter through some notes left in the language school. He was sub-renting the rooms in the flat in Via Bolognese. He was a student at the university, and was trying to finish his doctorate. After having lived in Berlin, he had got stuck living in Florence and couldn't leave the place. The same thing happened to me later on.

Peter had rented the Via Bolognese apartment from a woman who was a countess and a painter. The apartment had a wonderful view because it overlooked olive groves, and there were hardly any other buildings in sight. I liked the place and the people I lived with in this new place. Later on when we had to move, I continued to share a flat with Peter and Caterina, his girlfriend. We moved to Via delle Cinque Giornate (translates into: the five days of Milan str) in 1984.

Peter was sharing the flat in Via Bolognese with other young people; Janet, for example, was a Greek American girl from the Midwest, and she was engaged to be married to Paolo. She had a cat called Arturo and that is the reason we became fast friends almost immediately. Arturo had the use of all the rooms, and he used to use the long corridor for running sessions.

We could hear him at times when he was energetic and frisky, because during his race from one end of the corridor to the other he inexplicably jumped off the walls leaving paw prints there. It was one of those mysterious cat behaviourisms. It must have been fun for him to jump off the wall. He used to genuinely enjoy the thrill, as if he were a boy riding a skateboard! We used to comment on him doing this thinking that he did this as a compensation for his need to climb trees! God only knows what he was thinking.

Then there was the English boy called James, who had

managed to get his doctorate degree and he was looking for someone to replace him in the apartment. I was one of the people who turned up, asking to take the room which was free. James was going back to London. This room was the closest to the front door near the small room – i.e. "the maid's room" – which people used as a deposit for suitcases.

This small maid's room set off my imagination. It seemed that before the Second World War, people still worked as maids here in Europe, whereas now it was only the very wealthy who had live-in maids. In Asia people were still using such rooms, as the class of a maid and her social status still existed. I had seen it in Karachi, where it was usual to have help in the house. Even in Iran, women from villages found employment in private houses. I doubt that in Asian countries they would get a room all to themselves, however small it may have been.

The other girl staying there was a girl from Sardinia, and she was hardly ever in. She wasn't a student and was working in a bar and was very busy. The one time I met her, she told me without any preliminaries, "You are suffering from "culture shock". I was speechless when she said this, because we were meeting for the first – and the last – time and it seemed unnecessary for her to psychoanalyse my situation in five minutes and say it to my face as well.

This made me think that she was a witch and a bitch at the same time, but perhaps she was being kind and wanted to help me understand. It was a very alien attitude, and I wanted to tell her, "if you mind your own business a bit more, darling, you wouldn't have to work 10 hours a day!". However, I didn't open my mouth because I couldn't be bothered. Later on, I found out that what I had been subjected to was the "radiografia" – i.e. X-ray.

James was still staying in the apartment when I moved in. He was waiting for some time before he actually left Florence. I was really elated to be in the company of university students who were so far up in the ranks. They had a different attitude; it was as if the world belonged to them and they could demand for things to be given them. They only had to go out there and do things to get a good life. They were not into personal comments at all, even though once in a while some visitor would ask me what we produced in the country where I came from, which of course meant that I had to admit that I was from a country which was not yet industrialised.

Sometimes a political discussion would get off the ground, like one I had with James about Sabra and Shatila. It was 1983 or 1984 when this happened. I was very touched by what was happening there and I couldn't believe how Europeans were so much in favour of sitting at a table to discuss things, which only meant that no fighting was allowed and people were simply supposed to accept being defeated by the more powerful forces who were all for Israel, no matter what happened to the Palestinians.

Later on, James met my mother, and more discussions followed. He was then telling Peter about my mother being a very well informed person. It was a surprise to them that women from our part of the world should be able to talk about the politics of the region we came from, i.e. the Middle East with passion. Later on I came to think that perhaps in Europe passion was only allowed in small doses in normal life; people here usually didn't take things as seriously as we did, and perhaps that was a good thing.

Perhaps people would have strong feelings for football and other sports matches, or for music, and of course it was cute to have it in your relationships, but politics? I suppose that was why the Spanish were considered to be a passionate people in Europe because they could have political opinions, and that was why they had the Civil War, for better or worse.

At this time Caterina, Peter's girlfriend from Naples, was telling me that James had been living on fried eggs for months and that was why he had got through his degree. He had to save because he had very little money, and he had put all his energies and resources into his project.

Peter and Caterina were good together. Once we were preparing food in the kitchen and talking about our lives. Caterina was a very sociable, fun type of person to be with. I was twenty-five and thinking about getting a degree, whereas

Caterina, who was thirty-two, was asking me in a confidential way in her "napoletano" dialect, which I was capable of understanding, earnestly and in a very expressive manner, "ma io questi figli quando li devo fare?" which translates as, "at this rate, when am I supposed to have children?" She was thinking about creating a family; however, she knew well that it was difficult for her partner to settle into the Italian way of life.

The Italian way of life meant that if you didn't have money already, you were never going to make any in Italy unless you were a genius. Even to buy a small modest apartment was an achievement, and I admired people who managed to do this using their own capabilities. Later on I met Matthew, who was teaching English at university, and got his apartment by taking out a loan from the UK. I thought how lucky my parents had been to move to Iran in the fifties when, along with a lot of other people from various countries, they managed to get a loan and buy their own family home.

Sometimes when everything comes together with the right ingredients and at the right time, a miracle happens. My parents had left India due to the separation of India and Pakistan, and had then left Pakistan after a few years and had started a new life in Iran. They could barely speak the Farsi language. However, thanks to the Shah[8] – during his regime people could get mortgages – and the demand for Middle Eastern oil at the time, and thanks to their education and good, well-wishing Iranian friends – the population of the country was 30 million and not the 70 million it is today – they eventually found a steady occupation in the ministry and managed to put their education to some use.

The work situation was not promising in Italy in the 1980s, and you had to get in with the right circles in order to find suitable jobs. I could see it in Guido's family, where it was through connections that people got 'real paying' jobs. I suppose that was why Peter decided upon a career in Africa,

---

[8] The Shah of Persia was the last king of Iran ousted by the religious leader Ayatollah Khomeini, who spent many years as a refugee in France.

rather than getting married and settling down in Italy. I thought that was adventurous, but later on I found out that a lot of people left Europe in order to find work in less developed countries because the fact was that in Europe the job market was saturated.

One person who did get married was Janet. She and her fiancé Paolo got married in the red room in the town hall, and later on we all went to a house in the country to celebrate. In a typical silly way some people would whine and ask Janet, "but what is his mother going to do now without Paolo?", and she would reply dryly, "she'll live!" Janet was tough in a way, because she would be good at putting people in their place if they annoyed her – something I always admired, because I always thought about an answer years later!

My aunt and my cousin Farid came to visit me in 1984, when I was living in Via Bolognese. Janet really liked Farid and she told me I should leave Italy and return to my own family. I suppose, she had seen something of the truth of how difficult it was for me, as she was a down to earth American from Ohio.

I really liked the young people who, like myself, were trying to find a way to build their future, and I was happy to have left the life I had led in the centre. It had been the right thing to do. These people and their sense of solidarity and friendship meant a lot to me; however at times, there were some unnecessary frictions. Janet was always criticising Peter. In a way, all the Americans I met at that time had something to say about the Germans.

I didn't think that was fair at all. I could imagine how stressful it must have been to carry the burden of a country because I was experiencing it myself, having to put up with being categorised as an Iranian, which was not a good feeling after the revolution and the Iran/Iraq war. As if I had to answer for what was happening in my country. For instance, once at the hairdressers near work, I was getting a haircut and the man who was doing the work was saying, "Oh Iran! It is one of those countries on the news all the time! There is lots of trouble over there, while we live here in peace like good children!" Of course, it was my fault for not knowing what to say, and I continued to be sat upon in many occasions.

My cousin Ameneh, Peter and Guido

It was natural that I felt a sense of loyalty, because I had found this wonderful apartment and was living in it because of Peter's initiative. Actually, I respected Peter even though he had decided against my renting the room and joining them. How and why he changed his mind and later allowed me to stay, I don't know. Perhaps it was because Janet and James had said something in my favour.

Via Bolognese was a really enjoyable experience, except for my aunt's visit, which was sad.

I had told my aunt that I had proposed to my cousin during my last months in the UK. I had finally had the courage of speaking out because I saw she couldn't understand why me and my mother were hanging around in Karachi for months in her house. I realised that the time was not appropriate. Then I had left for Italy, seeing that I had created a lot of confusion and it was not getting cleared up in any way. Why hadn't I realised that many families were looking at my cousin as

God's gift to their girls?

She and my cousin were not happy to see me in the position I was in – I mean working as a saleswoman and living with total strangers. It could have all gone differently. Had the time been right, and if I had been lucky, I would have settled down to a regular life among my own people. But in Iran, a revolution burst out of nowhere and then a war with the neighbouring Iraq. The equilibrium was gone, and my confusion had bought me to bitter tears many times. How lucky you are to know the situation and the people you are dealing with. Today, I can see my cousin's point of view; I was a nice Iranian girl, but I wasn't really attractive or sexy or interesting. Some girls I have met are all that, without even having had an education. It was probably a cultural difference and attitude. In Iran and other Islamic countries, it is enough for a girl to be nice and from a good family. But in the West, it is more complex.

My cousin was much sought after by people in the family, and I was probably the last one on his list; contrary to his ideal of himself, I thought that I could save him from going away from his roots, but he probably didn't need my help!

The River
Watercolour Print, 2000

Today, my cousin is married to one of his ex-students, from a normal down to earth English family. They have a beautiful son and I am happy for them. I am sure that if I had had my way, I would never have been happy with them. More tears – and I am glad we didn't get together because we are simply very different – would be the consequence of that choice.

Moving To Via delle Cinque Giornate

My move to Via delle Cinque Giornate to the apartment of Mr Quercioli with Peter, was accompanied by Guido, Janet and Paolo, who had become my best friends. Paolo was a nice serious family man, an accountant, and he was solid and reliable. He was of our generation. Guido from Rome was of the 1968 generation, who went through the hippy type fashions. The Cultural Revolution that took place in Europe during 1968 turned out to be very positive – i.e. men really started to take women seriously. However, many people were confused in their ideas about life and about who they were and what they wanted.

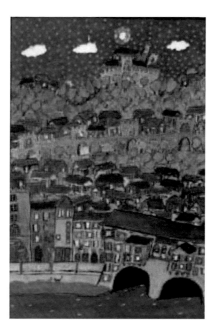

The Bridge
Watercolour, 2001

My Uncle Ismile, who was similar to Guido had seen the 1960s turmoil and they were both similar in their ideas. My uncle had met Guido in the Via Maggio apartment. He wasn't worried about Guido, but he was disgusted with the nice bourgeois place I had rented. He thought that I should be living in a students' pad. He didn't mind Guido, because he thought that they could understand each other. At some point in life, you realise that most people really do not care for other people that much, and when you have experienced lots of life, you realise that there is a limit to your family and friends caring about you.

You think that your family care for you deeply. But it isn't that way at all. Most of mankind is quite incapable of feelings. It is religion, philosophy and art that bring out the best in humans and even these fail horribly most of the time.

I realised this when I came back from Karachi to London in 1981, in order to get back to studying in Cambridge at the course which I had paid for. I was given a very hard time at Heathrow by an officer who said that they had read my private diary, which was in my purse. I was accused of wanting to stay in England and wanting to find a job. It was the year of the Iranian Revolution and before leaving the UK, I had been told that if I stayed in the UK for three years I would receive a British passport, but if I left, the conditions would be different.

I had needed to see my family more than anything else, and I had let the opportunity of a lifetime pass by. The right wing government was doing its duty and sifting out the people it didn't want.

The Sitting Room with Photographs
Watercolour, 2005

My uncle didn't care about me staying on, and so he let me go back to Karachi without any resistance to this new development. One nice English woman came to me and said that we could appeal against the decision. She was at least sympathetic, but I was feeling that I would probably burden my uncle with my presence.

Anyway, I liked Karachi and all the new people that I had met there. In Iran, there was the revolution and the war with Iraq, so staying in Pakistan with my aunt seemed to be the only solution. Later, I left Pakistan and the prospects of getting married and settling down there to return to Europe in order to go to university in Italy. That was my decision.

Sitting Room
Watercolour, 2007

Having lived in Via Maggio and then the Via Bolognese apartments, I now moved to the Via delle Cinque Giornate apartment. I was happy to move back to the centre, because I felt that was sort of a protection. I knew that Peter would soon sort out his doctorate and go to work somewhere in Africa. I thought it was an okay solution to find a place to live for my project of going back to university. I was really adamant about getting a degree, because I had been slighted by people for not having one. I thought that if I had a degree, I could defend myself the way my mother used to defend herself in society.

She had an MA in English Literature and started working when she was twenty three. She taught me that a woman had to fight in order to get somewhere in society, and education was very helpful for this. Though many believed this to be true, however being respectably married was the easiest way to social respectability for single woman.

I had four aunts, my father's sisters, who didn't get married. Homa was a nurse who had studied in the UK after the Second World War, Maheen was a librarian who lived away from the family in Shiraz, and the youngest of the eight children, Tahmeen, was a secretary who was living with her father. She drove a cream coloured Volkswagen around town and travelled abroad on her own. She tried to keep high standards and compensate for the problem child of the family who was Aunty Parveen. Parveen was the madwoman in the attic; she roamed the streets of Tehran with a very focused expression as if she knew exactly what she was doing, but she was perhaps autistic[9], or schizophrenic. Nobody really knew for sure. She was not lucky enough to be born when people knew a bit more about such ailments.

Her father had not wanted to put her in an asylum and had made his other daughters look after their sister. My aunts managed to survive by having a strong personality, and they looked after their sister in their newly adopted country. They had been brought up in India and now were in a new country, where getting respect in male dominated culture was a struggle as it ever was.

I still see family and friends in my dreams. These people, Janet, James, Guido and Peter too. Peter found a job with the United Nations Organisation and went off to Africa; I think to the Congo. I thought it was brave to make a move and do something new, rather than settle down to an unsatisfying situation. He left the Via delle Cinque Gironate apartment to me and said, "Why don't you rent the rooms if you need the money?" He was being practical. I had just enrolled in the university for a degree course in English and German Language and Literature. I could work and study at the same time.

---

[9] *Temple Grandin* is a wonderful film about autism and it made me take an interest in this Aunt who nobody wanted to remember. She had a sensitive expression and it was as if she was sorry to be a burden on her sisters. She got into tempers which we heard were terrifying for people who didn't know her. Her situation seemed hopeless at the time.

Working on the Old Bridge

It was 1984 and 1985. I was twenty-five years old and working at Ricci's Jewellery store on the Ponte Vecchio. I really wanted to be a student at the university, otherwise I was just another foreign shop assistant looking to settle down in Florence. I had left my job as a sales assistant in Maria Grazia's exclusive leather store because I felt very oppressed in that exclusively "business environment". Maria Grazia, the owner, was a very charming woman.

She would ask me, "Why do you buy a newspaper in Italian if you can't read it?"

I used to buy *La Republica* every day and look at the pictures and read the titles. I yearned for the day when I could master the language enough to be able to understand Italian like I understood English.

The Confused Couple
Oil on canvas, 2006

In Maria Grazia's opinion, my buying the newspaper daily was a waste of money because I couldn't read Italian. She was the store's owner, a petite attractive woman with a huge voice and lots of sentiment. She had a very tall husband called Lorenzo. They were very clever in their business, and I learnt a great deal of her attitude towards selling things. I was keen to learn from her, because she was full of vitality, good fun and very creative in her attitude towards life. However her son, who was my age, had some small issues with his parents, which was a sore point and made her compare me with her son. The poor guy had a lot of pressure on him because he was an only child, and I could understand why he was trying to do everything in order to please his parents.

The Soprano
Watercolour, 2007

Families are sometimes suffocating, especially when parents demand that their children be successful, like other people they know, without considering all angles of the picture. I could see how the conservative attitude of this couple was getting a bit too much. They reminded me of my own parents.

My parents too had always been looking towards other people's children and their achievements. Being an Iranian and non-European worked against me as far as finding another job was concerned. People's attitudes were so different here, and an education[10] didn't seem to count for much. When I told them that I would like to go to university, they said that no one ever made money by studying, and that degrees are all well and fine but are useless in life.

My friend Janet, too, had said, "Oh Boy!" – i.e. that university at twenty-five meant a huge amount of work, and for what?

I felt there was a repressive air which overlooked all youthful spontaneous joyous impulses towards the open sky. Some people wanted you to look down at your plate and never look up from it. Was it because if you looked up, you might get ideas of going after a better life? They seemed to want to keep you in your place. They seemed to want to fix you like a butterfly by pinning you down in the situation you find yourself in. That was how it felt for me and sometimes people didn't even want you to buy an intelligent and ambitious looking magazine. I found I was getting too stressed out and I had started to look for a new place and finally found a job where I was less involved with the managers.

I had found a place on the old bridge, which seemed very professional. However, after a while they let me go, saying that they were looking for a European.

Through a Dutch friend's contact, I had started working in a new shop selling jewellery on the Ponte Vecchio.

---

[10] " An Education" a coming of age drama, a film directed by Lone Scherfig in 2010 talks about the importance of a sentimental education as well as a "higher education". You wonder what would have happened if she hadn't recovered from that experience.

Casa A Serpiolle
Watercolour, 1999

Mr Ricci[11] Senior was never in the shop. He was a sixty year old with a sensitive expression. He liked women and was rather tuned in to the female mind. He had been a pianist in the past and so that was why the whole establishment had an air of old money and refinement. It was Daniele, his very tall son, who ran the place each day. He was a giant, one of those people who genetically are huge, but he was well proportioned.

Daniele used to put a nickname to all the people he knew. One guy who came into the shop to sell things, was called 'Piombo' (which translates into heavy metal) because he was very depressing. I was nicknamed 'Fenomeno' – i.e. not normal – which I thought was very flattering. But, I don't know if it was meant well, because sometimes his snootiness

---

[11] He had two lovely daughters in their twenties, who were kind and friendly. One of them who was in her early twenties and a gorgeous blonde shared the same girly issues with the rest of us, (Anna) she became a friend in later years.

came out at the most unexpected situations. Rosanna was the manager of the girls. She was about fortyish and was always knitting beautiful jumpers. I was grateful for not being directly under the owners like in the other shop.

The view from the window at Ponte Vecchio was gorgeous, but the shop didn't have a bathroom so people had to go to the cafes in order to use the loo. There were many rowing boats belonging to the boat club on the Arno. It was as if the people in the boat club were sitting on the beach in the middle of the town centre, very much like what they have in Paris today. In contrast to this, during the early 1980's, artisan and hippy type people used to sell their things on the bridge.

**The Bridge
watercolour, 2002**

There were lots of artisans on the old bridge. But in later years, all these people were removed. There was a lot of drugs going around as well, I think. I never really saw the drug culture, but later on in 2005 I was to know Michelangelo, Sandra and Marina's story, who was affected by drugs. For many years, I wasn't aware of it being such a threat to a lot of young people. For me, I would finish work and get back home by bus, always seeing the same faces of the people who lived in Via Bolognese. I would wonder who they were and how they used to live their lives.

That area, the old bridge, had an air of old families, country people and good wholesome energies, just like the families I had known. I was so happy that the Ricci's were nice people, not controlling and not the types to put you down.

Paintings belonging to this period

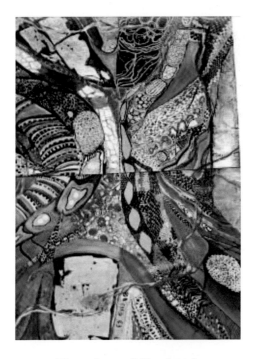

Energies and Tendencies
Oil on canvas, 1993-94

Energies and Tendencies is a painting that was sold in Dubai by a person who worked in Mondo Art Gallery.

I loved living in the spring 14 area of Dubai. It was a very special place, with lots of families with young children. It used to be fun to go out and see everyone who lived there doing their thing. This was a very nice area where people seemed to be well off. I had hoped to move here with my mother, but she wasn't destined to see this place.

Dubai has many different faces to it, after I left the villa, I had taken on rent in the Spring area. I still visited Dubai often and stayed in hotels.

I had to leave my house in Tehran often because of the pressures from the anonymous people. Perhaps some property developers had a plan to get rid of all the people who were living alone in big houses like myself. I had seen people sitting in the streets just watching, who came in and out of such houses. If you were not in the house then it was inevitable that your belongings would not be protected, because these people seemed to be able to get in one way or the other. Once I had gone to the police, and the man in charge had told me blatantly that I had to employ someone to watch the place when I wasn't there.

The same sort of thing had happened to me in Via Fiesolana in Florence. That is why I had my assistants there all day, and I was working hard to pay the bills. But I could never understand what was going on and why this was happening. I was very surprised to find the same thing happening in Tehran. Once when my mother was alive and we were living in the Tehransar apartment, I had left her on her own and gone out shopping, and when I came back she said that there had been a young man dressed in military clothes who had come in on his own accord and sat there with her for a while. He had then gone away without saying a word.

Now after my mother passed away I was on my own and I didn't want to live in Tehran. I had seen a group of nervous people waiting in a car. It seemed they were paid to do a job, and I was appalled by what was going on. They were waiting for their turn to enter an apartment, and who knows do what. It was the new world order at work; what they call the survival of the fittest. A woman I had met in Berlin, Suzanne, had asked me with a mischievous smile, "How is it in your area, and do you get on with the people?" Now I realised what she had meant. Whatever the plan was, it was probably European.

Dubai was, to say the least, a liberation. Someone had told me in Tehran that if you prayed three hours a day things would change for you. Three hours! It was an expression meaning a long time… Why I was putting myself through this type of life was because I simply wanted to sell my place and go away, but I had been tricked by a man who had said he would buy my house, and had then not paid me. It took me two years to take him to court, after which I realised that it had all been planned to a T and that he was only part of a huge machine all geared and heading towards some people's plan on making a big profit on the sale of my property.

Even the lawyers knew about it. One young thirty year old lawyer had told me that my case really didn't look good, because I had to pay very high court fees. Another less experienced lawyer had told me that he would pay the court fees himself, and this made me decide to stay on and fight the case. It was a losing battle, since his generosity and goodwill didn't have any results. I had waited two years to get my house back from a buyer who refused to pay me, and my lawyer had disappeared and gone on a trip to the US, and had no intention of fighting the case in court because he himself knew it was a game that was going to result in me having to pay the man – who was supposed to pay me – and a lot of other useless middle people. After all, it was the survival of the fittest and I was not strong enough to protect what I had rightfully inherited from my parents.

On the day we went to court, the judge, who was a surprisingly young man, stuck out his tongue; it was obvious that I was wasting my time, dreaming of having justice done.

I don't blame it on the women's condition in Iran. This was an international plan. Later on I heard about other people who had had to go through the same pressures. The buyer, had told me himself in one of our arguments that even God himself could not rescue me now. His partner, who said his Islamic prayers but was duping people as well, said to me that all the words I uttered would be used against me.

He even said that to my first lawyer, who quit after several attempts of talking to them. They had told him that they would peruse him and reveal things about him which were personal, which would certainly put him to shame. He gave up fighting for my case after I had had to put up with him for several months. The poor man seemed to have to scratch his balls every time he was introduced to people. He embarrassed me, but he had a heart of gold and I know that it was the times we were living in that made people misbehave. After all, what had anyone to lose when I was a person on her own?

So why was it that Sharon had come to Via Fiesolana to visit me in 2003, and telling me that such a thing would happen to me in 2008? Was it because she was a Zionist and a Communist? I wonder. This type of prophecy was to become a sort of constant element in my life from then on. Some people simply knew what was going to happen next. That Communists had a part in all this was clear. It seemed to me that Iran was a satellite, or was on the way to becoming one, of its powerful neighbour, who was installing nuclear energy. Was it them who were doing this?

I had read in the English papers of a bizarre happening in London, where an old man who was living in a big house in an expensive location was harassed by a man from an ex-Communist state, who later claimed to have inherited the place. It seemed that some people wanted to get money effortlessly; another lawyer told me that "they simply were plucking the fruit from the tree", and didn't intend to do any harm to the tree itself.

A lot of people had to feel happy with that explanation.

That is why my trips to Dubai took me to a country which was a sort of holiday haven. I wish I had discovered Dubai before going to Italy, because it was a much better place in the eighties, and people I met who had settled there in those years were now well off and lived a relaxed lifestyle. I had met Linda, who was English, in Florence, and she had told me that she'd lived in Dubai in those years. Now I realised that she had been so much more experienced than many of the people I met in Italy.

I had found the Mondo Art Gallery in the mall of the Emirates whilst I was living in the Spring 14 area in a villa I had rented in Dubai in 2007. I had actually gone to the mall that day to meet Olivier, who was an estate agent. We met in a café and he showed me some pictures of houses on his laptop, pictures of properties. My mother had just passed away and I was thinking about moving back to Italy. I had to sell my parents' house in Tehran in order to buy a new place. After meeting the estate agent, I went to the Mondo Art Gallery in the mall to check it out.

I had always intended to go in and introduce myself, and this is how I met A, who was the manager of the gallery.

I walked in, and she was sitting there with a tense expression on her face, which wasn't welcoming or pleasant. She looked rather on guard and cross. However, I got up the courage to go up to her desk and talk to her. I spoke to her in Italian and she was nice; she told me that she would come to my house and see my work, since she was living in a villa close to mine. My canvases were at home now, as I had got them sent over from Italy. This was before I had to leave Dubai due to the problems with the sale of my property.

In Florence, Sara had asked her singing colleague Anne to help me with my belongings, which I had had to leave behind. Anne had been kind and had kept them in the basement of the building, which belonged to the Evangelist church. They were kept there for an entire year. I had gone to Florence to get these things packed and sent to Dubai, with the intention of living in Dubai, eventually selling my house in Tehran and moving out of Iran. I told A about my plans of selling my house in Tehran. Probably that was a mistake. I wasn't aware that the microphones were hiding very unscrupulous people behind them.

People's interest in selling my property seemed weird. It wasn't the normal type of interest as it had a predatory feel about it. Perhaps some people had been fleecing the population in the middle east for many years, through these methods of collecting information – i.e. security and control with microphones and CCTV. Someone was war mongering in the Middle Eastern property market in this way for ages. How

81

naïve of me to have made the mistake of saying anything about the sale of my property to anyone at all.

A was a woman from northern Italy, and she selected some of my paintings and held an exhibition of them for two weeks. She managed to sell this painting called 'Energies and Tendencies' to a man who, she said, bought the painting because he liked her! I appreciated the energy she put into talking about my paintings to the clients. She really did put her heart and soul into her work, and was very stressed out most of the time. She had to quit the job several months later.

The painting 'Energies and Tendencies' was about Iran and the Middle East. I had purposely not hung the two canvases on the wall the way they are supposed to be hung, because I was afraid that the outline of the map of Iran would become an issue with people viewing it in the gallery.

The two panels, if stuck together the right way, would give an outline in white and red, which was the "cat like" outline of the map of Iran. I hadn't meant to do a picture about Iran, but there was so much going on in the picture, that I thought, "Hey! This looks like a turbulent mess, like the Middle East". Then there are drawings of the cell division, which meant new births and new mutations and new life and everything, because that was what was happening in Iran and the Arab countries of the region. Perhaps there is energy in the Middle East because of the ongoing struggle to survive.

Energies and Tendencies (Detail)
Oil on canvas
Life in Dubai and Tehran 2007

There are flowing colours, because I wanted to show the
undercurrents to our political situation. Whether Soviet
Russia's influences through the indoctrination of young minds
or America's influence, everyone was in Iran undercover.
Even China was now courting Iran, because after the war with
Iraq there was a whole country just waiting to be rebuilt from
scratch.

However, the Middle East is unstable because we have too
many pressures from the outside and are never left in peace to
develop as we need to do. Our culture and traditional ways

don't help us get organised because they are manipulated by foreign powers all the time. Who knows if the person that bought this painting knows what I meant to say, but I am sure that he liked the detailed state of confusion depicted in it.

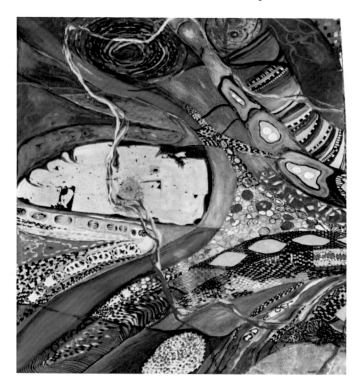

Detail of 'Energies and Tendencies'

I selfishly wish there had been no revolution in the country where I was born, so that my life would not have had to change. The revolution had some positive points, but it had made us easy prey to the countries whose people had no fear of God. While we were praying away, they worshipped the "golden calf", and were getting away with doing this at our expense. They were the new gods, operating from behind the scenes, they were holding onto the strings of our lives and they really could not and did not care for the suffering they caused. I can testify to many young people committing suicide or dying of heart attacks in Tehran for the rough use of this new invisible "stasi power".

I can imagine that the elitist control practiced by the security forces behind the CCTV and the microphones – their treatment of people's private lives as their personal serfdom – to be one of the reasons for revolt in the middle east. In the month of Ramadan in August 2011 in Syria, people are going out every Friday to meet their deaths with no fear. How far have they been pushed to not want to live?

After the revolution in Iran, universities closed in the country and a negative view of Iranians took hold and flourished due to the US hostages of the Embassy, and then the Iran/Iraq war. And now the control of Stalinists with their Stasi methods. How bad could it get for us Iranians who were trying to live out our little lives like everybody else? Having lost all our privileges from one day to the next, who could be happy in this new situation?

My own life tossed about like a little boat on the ocean waves, destiny had come to put us in our place. We were once again a tribal people, just as we had always been. The citizen mentality of Western Europe, which was what we aspired to, was still an ideal to be reached. The population went from thirty million to seventy million, and the new generation was bought up on other values – hence the name 'Energies and Tendencies' – a new era had begun for all of us.

One good thing that came out of the revolution was that we no longer had a stuffy Asian class system which saw people stuck in the social status they were born into. The Arab Spring in 2011 was about similar issues. Work and the working classes were finally discovered.

Today in 2009, the 1st of November, Iran is negotiating with the West, trying to be accepted by the world as a nuclear country. The many years of war in Iraq and Afghanistan, and the problems in Pakistan are being kept at bay – here in Iran perhaps, by the prayers of our saintly people?. Even today, the stability in Iran is a miracle.

In the poem 'Out There', I want to give the message to people who want to do something in their lives to just do it, procrastinating because you feel tied by feelings for others is useless. You have to try your luck one way or the other, because the individual can be overwhelmed by the immensity of the things that are going on. This is a tribute to all the people who take that boat and come out trying to cross the waters in order to seek a better future somewhere else. You risk your life and no one can guarantee anything.

Al Noor, oil on canvas, 1989
From the Holy Koran
The Chapter Al Noor (meaning Light) v.35, 36
*"God is the light of the heavens and the earth, his light is like
this: there is a niche, and in it a lamp, the lamp inside a glass, a
glass like a glittering star, fuelled from a blessed olive tree from
neither east or west, whose oil almost gives light even when no
fire touches it – light upon light- God guides whoever he will to
his light; God draws such comparisons for people; god has full
knowledge of everything"*

4. Al-Noor

This is one of the first paintings, which I find has balance and
equilibrium. The point is that when one paints abstract
paintings without having a direction, the painting is an
adventure and happens on its own. It isn't an action painting,
because this intuitive painting has certain guidelines and isn't
totally left to chance like action painting. Rather, it is an image

which you have inside of you, and you project it on the canvas – fishing it out, as it were. I remember that was what some romantic painters thought of painting; the image was there in your subconscious mind somewhere and it just had to be captured.

This painting I called 'Noor' – i.e. 'light'. But it is very dark and only the centre yellow patch can justify it being called light, meaning that in a world of darkness and confusion, when there is light, things have outlines and one can distinguish ones surroundings; that is what light does.

This is a very stern image, really earthy with the browns and the greens, and it reminds me that mother nature is rough and unkind most of the time. Mankind is perishable and nature has always been a force which he has had to struggle with in order to survive. The prospect of death and disease has always made men and women search for ways to prolong their stay on earth. Centuries have passed with humans clinging on to gods of one kind or the other before coming up with the concept of an abstract God. One wonders why humans have been and are so materialistic. And yet, they have reached a point of abstraction.

But then there is that something which is unfathomable and ethereal in this painting. In the midst of the heavy as it were; down pulling weight of reality. Light is uplifting in a miraculous way. It can fly above the flesh and the sinews and the issues of being alive on this earthly dimension.

It is as if I were walking with my soul hanging out for water; I walk the desert dehydrated as a plant and then all of a sudden, I come to an oasis where there is water and the safety of the trees and vegetation. This an analogy to our spiritual need for hope in a difficult world, described so well in the first chapters of the novel *The Source* or *Hawaii*, written by James Michener, where humans would do anything to have rain falls or to keep negative times and situations at bay.

Noor, the light, is hope, and it is also good news, a sort of light at the end of the tunnel; a gift from God the creator, who declares himself a friend of the believers.

I have written the verse from the Holy Koran around it in a Persian, which is not at all refined. It is more the handwriting of a child. This is because I wanted to represent an every man or woman who is not necessarily refined, or even educated. Perhaps because I think God isn't classist or sexist and appreciates the heartfelt feelings of the believers.

The verse describes the feeling of light – i.e. of God's presence. It is such a mysterious way of comparing the light of God to a light of something material. The light of God would be like this, it says, rather than describing God itself.

"God is the light of the heavens and the earth. His light may be compared to a niche that enshrines a lamp".

This painting was given as a gift to my childhood friend. Today in August 2011, there is the prospect of famine in Somalia. People have lost their animals and thousands are leaving their villages in order to take refuge in and around cities. It is a hopeless situation. Who can sustain these thousands, and for how long? It reminds you of the biblical stories about Egypt and the story of the Prophet Joseph. The seven lean years have perhaps returned.

Sharon &Sara

"Momenti Brillanti"
(which translates to "Life's Brilliant Moments")
mixed media on canvas, 1991

After the divorce, Sharon[12] had sold her house and had lots of millions in old lire in the bank. Now she was on her way to a new future. I'll never forget the little apartment she had bought in the Via delle Pergola, No. 50, in front of the hospital, because I had spent some days staying there. I wished that I was as practically minded as she was. She could organise her life, and even having a terrible private life didn't touch her

---

[12] As in the film 'Thelma and Louise' .... Sharon had bought a red Sports car and would give us a ride at times, which was very exhilarating.

deeply. How did she keep buoyant? After all, our emotional life is our ship which keeps us floating on life's ocean. My prayers were my way of navigating the waters of life. But what did she have? Relationships with people?

Piazza Santo Spirito, "because it has got soul"
Watercolour, 1998

The thing she did was to visit a psychologist, who seemed to have told her that our friendship was bound to fail. So, instead of saying, "I'm sorry if I hurt your feelings", she just continued on her way, dropping me out of her life. I'm sure I knew that this relationship/friendship would go like that. I hadn't altogether invested too much in it, as I knew I was going in a different direction.

I had liked her for her qualities, her sense of humour and her indefatigable energies in work and play different directions – so it was inevitable. However, we did have some good times before we fell out.

Piazza Santa Croce, And The Beloved Fluffies
Watercolour, 2002

I was working in a jewellery store in Piazza S Croce that summer, and she called me one day and said, "Why don't we go on holiday to Maremma together"? I was enthusiastic, but what was in the news then in 1993 and 1994 was that some people were throwing stones at moving cars on the Auto Strada. It was on the news all the time, and that made me afraid, but it didn't bother her. She had a new red sports car and we had been going around looking at houses for her to buy. I had volunteered to go with her, because I thought one day I might want to buy something in Italy. It was just to do something interesting and to be in her company. I was happy to have a friend from New York, because Sharon was interesting and of another background. We drove down to the Parco del Uccellino and had a little adventure in the countryside, trying to find a place to stay the night. We found this house in the country with a strange man who professed to be a witch doctor. It was very scary, to say the least. Going on that trip inspired me with very sad feelings.

I had a much more fun time with Sara and Eric. Even though they didn't have money, they had the spirit and were sort of innocent and had self-absorbed originality, and that is what makes fun. When they were preparing to go somewhere like a wedding, Eric would shout up to Sara to ask what she was going to wear with enthusiasm, as if it was of the greatest importance to him as well; what she wore and how she looked. Eric had lived in Pietra Santa, as he professed to be a sculpture.

I thought that Sara's living in Piazzas Spirito was the reason I found her exciting to be with, even though I had known her before that. But it was not that. The place contributed to the social life that she loved with all her singing friends. A lot of people sang in the church choirs like her. Through singing in the choirs and at weddings, she had become a known personality. In her own sphere, people knew her and she went to all the parties, which were the right ones.

**Houses In The Countryside, My Walks Around Via
Bolognese
Watercolour, 2003**

She hung out with the artists, or the aspiring ones. I think her attitude of working hard towards a goal was admirable. It really reminded me very much of a humble way a person in love approaches an unreachable beloved. She had made up her mind to enjoy whatever life gave her on her way to her goal, that had always been to become a professional soprano. Unlike Sharon, she wasn't at all demanding. How did she manage to do everything? I couldn't understand how she found the time to sleep, with the few hours that she got to be in her house. It was extraordinary! My life was certainly the laziest life of the three of us because I absolutely needed to sleep a lot. I had learnt to do that from Philippe, who was sort of a dormouse.

My mother too always said that it was best to sleep as much as one could when one got the chance to do it. Sharon and Sara however were not into wasting time sleeping at all. They both went jogging in the morning – ugh!

Sara, too, did these superwoman type things. But she really had a strong Latin sense of life as well. The Anglo Saxon part of running after achievements and being matter of fact was a part of her personality. She disliked Eric not having money and not working.

Pietra Santa, Piazza Del Paese
Watercolour, 2002

But she did like to be sociable and to be right in the middle of the action, and to know everybody in the world, especially the people who were the "in type". She was in with such a wide range of people through her singing friends. It was mind boggling how many people she knew and the circles she moved in.

But her heart was in the small intimate private life, and that wouldn't allow her to use relationships in order to move up socially. She couldn't be mercenary in her friendships, even if she wanted to. I suppose being an artist means that those heart issues and feelings are very important. I appreciated her being childlike in that sense. I think that we were similar in that way. In that, we hadn't lost that little girl inside, and that that child was still walking with us through our life, hindering us in some ways, but still making us look up in wonder at the stars in the night sky.

Eric was an idealist too and in that sense he liked Sara. One could tell that he was very irresponsible. He had lovely long hair, braided down his back Indian style, that made him look very romantic. Together with Marco the photographer, who looked like someone out of Led Zeppelin, they were a team of hippy type idealists. Did anyone I know work in Florence? A lot of people that I'd known in their thirties didn't really work at all. Many of them stayed at home and had no money. It required courage to go out there and participate in the world.

I had worked as a saleswoman, but preferred to rent out rooms like Marco had done for many years. It wasn't a healthy life at all, and people didn't respect that. Eric too was the type that wanted a good job, and not just any old type of work. He used to talk big about space and spaceships and it was top quality that he was after. It was refreshing to talk to someone who still hoped that good things could happen in the future. I think that it may be the pioneer spirit of the Americans that is so attractive. Because whilst Asians and Europeans are tied to the ground by their feudal history, always interested in who owns land and who doesn't, these new continent people I knew had a totally different attitude. The 'can do' attitude in Eric and Sara didn't last. There were too many people after Eric, and they didn't have the stamina to make it as a couple.

I mean Patriza[13], who had met Eric at a party at my house, fell for him. That was why Sara blamed the party at my house, for bringing Patriza and Eric together, resulting in Sara losing him. Sara then met Curro who was Spanish, into opera and owned a Harley Davidson type of motorbike.

---

[13] Patrizia a typical middle class girl who drove a nice jeep about town and for some reason reminded me of Mina the songwriter and performer.

"The Mermaids, An Underwater Fantasy"
Watercolour, 2007

He was working for a noble family in Florence, and was much more together than the rest of us. Eric was expensive, and Patriza had the money. She appreciated him because he was an American and in a sense different. She put up with a lot, because one could tell that Patriza and Eric worked really hard to keep up the relationship they had started. Patriza had always liked the idealist types and she was into nobility, like Eric's previous Italian girlfriend.

Socially it worked, and Patriza then went to the States with him. She became a better person having gone through that experience. One thing about Eric was that he did care about other people – his group, as it were. One day, after I had got my money – the 'reward', as Matthew called it – for doing the case against the jewellery shop in which I had been harassed, Eric came to Via delle Cinque Giornate on his own. He said to me, "You must start to work, because the money is going to soon disappear". He was right, because the money was only twenty million old Lire. I knew that if I paid all the rent money that I owed for the apartment, I could keep the apartment forever, according to the Italian laws then. However, I decided against this, as I didn't want to make the apartment, which wasn't mine, the centre of my life like Marco had done. It made me feel bad about what I was doing to the owners.

"I Was Going To Say That I Loved You, But I Found Out
That I Did Not Belong To Myself"
Mixed technique on canvas, 1989

"The Reunion Of Old Friends"
Pen and ink on paper, 1987

I thought that it was God's wrath upon me that I didn't feel happy with my life and couldn't find a way out of my problems. I thought about Nadia and how courageously she had lived and worked in the hotel as a receptionist for some years, but had decided to go back to France. She had made a strong decision and taken responsibility. Living with compromises makes one weak and tired. That is why I decided to let the apartment go and to eventually get evicted from it. I had lived in this apartment on the ground floor of Via delle Cinque Giornate, No. 6, for fifteen years.

"The Lovers"

"Room With View On The Persian Persepolis With
Traditional Woman"
Watercolour design on paper, 2002

I could have married somebody and settled down and had children. But that wasn't why I'd come to Europe at all. I had come to Europe because I wanted to become a person who produced good art, and achieving that was utmost on my mind. It was posterity that I was thinking of because I thought that all children in the world could be my children if I had a good message to give them. I disliked the idea of thinking about reproducing one's DNA in a world which had always been a difficult place. I mean, if I'd had the strength to do that, I would have had a family. But, I was usually the one that got hurt in relationships.

Mr X said that he thought of getting married, but that I would have to wait. No one was crazy enough to want to get married to someone like me! I thought of myself as being very depressing. I had lost the chance of my life, when Philippe had once politely asked about us getting engaged. I had been flippant about it and had ignored his serious words. He had always been very sweet so it was my own fault for not knowing what is was that I was after.

I spent the next ten years thinking about Philippe every day, and desiring to be with him in every relationship I had. Even when I was with Sara, Sharon, Mr X and Nadia, I was wishing to be with him. I was one person with two hearts. It was amazing, like having two photographs that didn't sit right together, even though they were the same. I thought about my Islamic background and how that would hinder me from being with anyone from the West. Also, how any Islamic man would hinder me from being free to grow as a person.

Santo Spirito & Sara & Marco

In any case, no one was asking me, "What is it that makes you feel happy because I want to make you feel happy or be part of your happiness". I recently saw that in a film[14] and I thought

---

[14] In later years I saw Indian films like "Hum Tum", or "Bride and Prejudice" or even "Come dancing"; which seemed to analyse relationships between the two sexes in a way which was close to my own mentality and I realised the romantic

I've always been so selfish and self-centred. I suppose I have never been out there trying to make anyone feel happy but myself. Only once in a surge of enthusiasm, which I couldn't understand myself, I thought that I could teach Mr X English and that would have made a difference in his life. But I thought it too much of a mad idea, and as he was so much into his own routine, it didn't seem to be realistic.

What am I, some sort of teacher? I thought to myself, that he talked about his friends at the market 'liking him just the way he was'. So I came to the conclusion that he wouldn't have tried to make an effort. The market stalls are where people fall in and out of relationships, and he had a lot of friends at work. He was saying how one Italian girl had come and sat on his lap one day and how they called him nicknames. I thought that there is so much that I don't know about this person and so much he isn't telling me – and so much he will never tell me.

I had a feeling that there was someone very important in his life, and that I wasn't such a hot item for him after all. Then I thought, well, I'll ask him to get married, and he knows how important that is. I can't be hanging around here waiting for him to decide, so I will have to go ahead and do my thing. As I guessed, he didn't pursue the issue much and we left it at that. That was in 1994, after my mother had come to visit me and I had told her about him. She met him and told me that he was a bright person who wouldn't stay in his social position but would go further. I thought that was so generous of her to say that – thank you Mum! I was really grateful that she was optimistic about him. But at the same time she said, "You know you must find someone who is from the same background". I don't know if she said "like us", but I think she meant educated. An education had been so important to myself, and to the people in my family. Even my uncle had got

---

ideas that I had about love and marriage had been talked about already in a comprehensive way. Especially in *Hum Tum* the story evolves between a cartoonist who has warped ideas about women and a girl who is traditional, and I can associate my point of view with the Karan's.

a degree at forty after having worked at the travel agency for many years.

He started to go to university late and got his BA, and then started to teach. I understood where she was coming from. Karina had told me some years back when we were sitting in Piazza Santa Spirito to go and talk to Philippe when he had approached me. But that was just before my degree, and I thought that I couldn't afford to get into an emotional tangle after such a lot of hard work. I had let him go. He had definitely been very important to me.

I realised that I had such an important thing to finish and that I would lose it if I kept running after people all the time. I had wanted to get a degree because of my parents as well. I suppose in order to make everyone happy. I had left home for this purpose and I was delivering what I said I would do. I am sure that my parents would have been much happier if I had brought children into this world and made a family for myself.

Life in post-revolutionary Iran had lowered the standards, and people didn't expect much from woman. Making a family was a prestigious achievement for a woman. In fact, after all my efforts for getting a degree, all my mother had to say was, "So you finally pulled yourself up to my level", which was a sign that my family weren't very impressed at all. I know that a BA degree is for when one is twenty three and not the age of thirty two. I had given up my happiness on the way, but I was happy that I had finally understood what was good for me.

My Swedish flatmate Karina, who was a very smart woman and who seemed to be observing my life, had also told me that I didn't seem to have much time to spend in a family or a relationship anyway. Even if I had wanted to, I had too many things that were important to me. She had been right. I was on my way to producing an art studio, and that needed all my strength and concentration. Philippe was important as an inspiration and I wish that I had had the strength to help other artists too.

Karina, Sharon and others had helped me on the way to establishing the studio; so had Mr X, so had Patrizia, Enzo, Paola, and Caterina.

It was a help to my survival, and so had many others. However, spiritually they hadn't given me the strength that Philippe had given me. Through him, I had found my identity as an individual and my forefathers and their dedication. He had been a source of energy as only some special people can be. When I was in his company I thought that everything was beautiful and intelligent, even plants, and everything had stronger colours.

It was as if I had taken enhancing drugs. I thought perhaps that it was the same sentiment. It felt like being in an Indian movie. As usual, I declared myself, it was in a coffee shop in Piazza Santa Maria Novella. It was raining hard. There was thunder and lightning like never before. I thought the weather was expressing my state of mind. All Indian movies have rainy scenes.

He said, "you are lying!" Then he took my arm. I had these gold bangles on and he examined them as if they were horrible things. It was as if he was thinking, these can't be real gold! How disgusting if they were! I was ashamed of my gold bangles then. My mother had bought them for me in Karachi in Pakistan. They were 22 carat gold, they weighed a lot and were worth a good sum. When he looked at them that way, I tried not to wear them anymore. In the West, people don't wear gold like we do in Asia or Africa. I saw the Somali girls sometimes wearing their gold with pride. Here I was, being cross-examined because of them, as if no one could understand the necessity of wearing such a lot of gold. It wasn't safe, I thought, so I put them in the bank and they were there for many years after that.

The declaration didn't go well as usual. He said, "why do you kill things as they are growing, and why are you such a rock?" I thought, I cannot very well change what I am. Then he said, I have an Israeli girlfriend that is slimmer than you, and on to the scene came the Israeli girl who was his best friend's wife! That was another story. I thought here I am being sincere, and he is playing games with me! I suppose it was a bit like what Picasso did with his women. Many years later, I read that Picasso used to make women fight over him in his presence and he enjoyed that.

What really was unpleasant then was that I didn't really have any money, and he was very sure that he didn't want a woman weighing on his life and on his pocket and he didn't want any problems. That was what he told me. At that point, I was sure that I didn't want any problems myself because I was just a few steps away from my last exams, and then I had to write my final paper. So I thought, okay, this is going to be tough, but I have to get out of this relationship.

I was thirty and I didn't want to waste any more time getting through my project. Later on Cristiana, who was modelling for Philippe, asked me, "I suppose you don't really believe in love?" She said that because maybe she would have dealt with the matter in a different way.

The Triangle of relationships

Cristiana had been married to a French man, and could speak French and Spanish fluently. She could understand Philippe on a different level. I said, well, I have to answer to my family and I can't throw everything away in the name of love. Here was all my family expecting me to give them a result, and I really didn't feel like letting them down for someone who really didn't care for me that much.

Plus there was competition from a slim Israeli woman, or perhaps many women, because he was an attractive thirty two year old, well-bred and a bachelor from a seemingly bourgeois family. I am sure he didn't get married to any of the women I saw him with after that.

The slim Israeli woman went on to have two children by her Italian painter fiancée. The man who was Philippe's friend, looked as if he walked out of a film about Italy in the 1800s. He had a huge, long, old-fashioned beard and didn't look like normal people – he reminded me of the Amish people in the US who still live without cars. He had taken a book out of his car, and I had commented how much I disliked the artist the book was about. I really hadn't expected my humble opinion to mean anything to him.

However, he was quite offended and told me that on the contrary he was an admirer of Giorgio Morandi, the painter who painted bottles. Canvas after canvas. I couldn't see the point of bottles being the subject of the paintings.

I hadn't realised that this man really liked Morandi. He seemed to be irremovably placid most of the time, but turned red all of a sudden when he heard my opinion. "How dare you say that?" he said, and he showed me a huge book of thousands of pages on his favourite painter. I was humbled by my mistake.

Morandi had spent the whole Second World War painting pictures at his home in the countryside. Perhaps the ugliness of the war makes us concentrate on the few things that we can control, which still are absolutely innocent and clean. Perhaps that was Morandi's message; he was saying, "I don't really like this reality but I will make up my own". He was such a charitable person, because later on people who had his paintings would become rich. I actually met an Italian couple who had bought an expensive apartment having sold one of his paintings.

Sara

Sara's[15] kitchen and her life, in a way, were my surrogate for wanting to be with Philippe. Sara was much like myself, trying so hard to make it to her goal. One can always get lost upon her way. Sara was one who was suffering for her cause, like myself. Right before she finally got though the exams, she and I met in front of the Santo Spirito church steps, and she was desperately crying, saying, "I know that I can sing I just have to make it through this".

I had never seen her so depressed. Making it meant lots of studying, lots of hard work at her piano and on top of that, working at her teaching job in order to make a living. Cristiana was another surrogate for Philippe. I became friends with her when she was modelling at the Charles Cecil Art School. She had long hair which she dyed blonde, and a very sexy gruff voice, which reminded of the actress Monica Vitti. She wanted people to think that she was sexy like Brigitte Bardot.

Cristiana wasn't really sexy at all when one got to know her as a person. I mean, she wasn't false and calculating. She was actually a nice girl from a nice family in northern Italy, who wanted to create a family with some guy. She told me that she had been married to a French man and had lived in France for some time. But now she was separated.

Cristiana had a studio in Via Guelfa, a really seedy part of town in the centre near the railway station. She painted copies of paintings by the masters. They were usually renaissance paintings, ones with lots of books and musical instruments and

---

[15] Sara and I felt a lot of affinity with the heroine of the film "The Girl With The Gun" (La ragazza Con La pistola) by the directer Monicelli which is a comedy from the 60's with the lovely actress Monica Vitti. It is about a girl from the outbacks of deep southern Italy who follows the man who she thinks she is in love with (who is running away from her) to London. She is transformed by the new world she discovers and the people she meets along the way. Eventually she becomes a successful model and develops a new side of her personality.

Persian carpets. I went to visit this apartment and studio often. I liked her paintings. She borrowed this art book from Philippe and really messed it up. It seemed as if she didn't care to hurt his feelings at all.

I would have had more respect for that book, whoever it had belonged to. However, Cristiana could get away with a lot, because she was a warm-hearted girl and she did have good intentions. Her voice, I found, was very attractive.

I had told her about my experience as a painter. I told her that I knew Philippe, and that is why she allowed me to go to her studio and she taught me how to use gold leaf. I felt that I should have paid her for it, only I didn't have any money to show her how grateful I was. She was one of the people in Florence who had been generous and nice and hadn't wanted anything back.

As luck would have it, she found a young Scottish girl who had tried to open a gallery in Florence, who had actually bought some of her canvases and paid for them up front! It was unbelievable. No one used to do such things in Florence – at least, no one we knew about. I asked this young gallery owner, "are you actually buying paintings with the idea of helping artists?", and she answered that it was incredible but true. I could feel that she had taken a huge burden upon herself.

In the meantime, whilst I was studying for my last exams, Cristiana had found a partner, Leonardo, who was a Florentine IT expert. He was living in an apartment right next to the Porcellino Square in the centre, and he had a degree in mathematics. Her fiancé was very much a leftist and a pleasant person, with a sense of humour. Cristiana had found him because she had gone to a party in the European University with a Dutch PhD student. Leonardo had asked her to dance, and she had dropped the student and had made friends with Leonardo.

Later on, they had two children and got married. It was unbelievable. I pitied the Dutch man, but it was typical.

Later on, she told me that she liked the men who wore suits and ties, but they were very demanding and were after women who had money. She didn't have money and she was looking for someone who wanted to have children and who could look after a family. She knew what she wanted. It was Cristiana who told me that some people could get special permission for getting a divorce from the pope, in order to get married to someone else.

I suppose those kinds of men in suits and ties like rich women like Patriza, who could afford to spend lots of money on fashionable clothes, who had a car – a new one – and an apartment, and a father who spent money on them. I hadn't realised that the money game was a worldwide thing. If a girl seemed not to have money, then she would probably not be able to pick and choose.

I looked at Cristiana with admiration because she was so much the woman who wanted to be very feminine, and she knew what was required of her – i.e. to be slim, to be blonde, to be flexible, to wear short skirts and appear sexy – such a lot of hard work! She was now thirty years old and had made up her mind that she wanted children and that this was the time to do it.

I was thinking how in the Middle East, woman have it easy in a sense, because families think of getting the young people married off through arranged marriages. No man or woman, however unattractive or poor, wastes time searching for the right partner. After all it is all about procreating the genes – so everyone, ugly or attractive, with defects or illnesses, rich or poor, educated or unemployed – everyone could get married because it was done as a social rule. But in Europe it seemed so difficult. People had to find the right partner and very few of my girlfriends ever did find the right people.

They actually had to go through various experiences and mistakes in order to settle for the least satisfying partner. In the Middle East, I was surprised that even people that couldn't afford to have children were having them and bringing them up somehow or other.

In the West, many planned to have kids but couldn't because having kids was expensive and you had to give up a comfortable life if you wanted to have a family. My Italian friends from university had their own homes and could afford to get married, but they took years to decide to settle down together seriously. A lot of woman I knew didn't find a partner at all, and just had a child with someone, just to enjoy being a mother. What worried everybody was finding a steady income; it was the 1990s, and things were not looking so good.

I was working at Piazza Santa Croce at a jewellery place in the summers, and there would be days when there was no one in the square. In the late 1980s, there had been a lot of Russians who had brought lots of money. They would carry lots of cash with them and invest it in gold. It was when the Soviet Union became Russia. It was 1988 and 1989, and Mr Gorbachev was on the news all the time with Glasnost and Perestroika being the key words in the news. It crossed my mind that Gorbachev wouldn't last long because he was a university professor, and too much of an idealist. Then the siege of the Palace happened and Yeltsin took over.

The shop where I worked was owned by an Italian family. The owner, who was Florentine was called Mr C. He had married a Russian women called Vera; she was nice looking then. She had big blue eyes and long frizzy hair and a very triangular face. She was very feminine. Soon she got to take part in the business in a big way, because all our clients were Russian. When she had worked in the shop for some years, she cut off all her hair and kept it really short, and she started to become masculine in her ways. I think it was because she was carrying more responsibility on her shoulders. She was very modest about her education, but she was an aeronautics engineer. She use to talk about Moscow and it was fascinating for me and my colleague Nora to listen to her stories of life before Italy. Right then, there were a lot of Russians coming over to Italy, who were on their way to the states. Anja gave them hospitality and one of her Jewish guests who hadn't a penny and used to sleep in the car, later on went to New York and became very rich. According to her, he had established several supermarkets there. Something big was happening, and we were unaware of what was brewing in the pot.

"The Australian Belief in Dream Time"
Mixed media, 1988

Cell phones had just come out, and Anja had one. It was very such a fashionable thing to be seen trotting about with a phone pressed close to the ear. This made one feel rich and important, because not many people had one. The cheap ones were huge and heavy things which had batteries that didn't last long at all. The mobile revolution was just beginning but answering machines were still an item of importance, remaining from the 1980s. Sharon, in her new wealthy situation, had bought one of those new phone/fax machines, which had everything including an answering machine.

De La Soul, the band, was really in vogue because of the bit in the song with the beep of the answering machine. It was very hip. We used to read about Yeltsin and his drinking habits. The Russians were educated and cultured, but were stuck with these leaders, who failed to deliver stability to their country. Moscow was supposedly a terrible place to live in; we heard about the poor and the old – i.e. people who had been used to a welfare state; they couldn't adapt to the new pace of life. There was news that the youth were forming gangs, and that was making life very difficult for the ordinary citizens.

It was Russia in the limelight, and Anja was a real Russian from that planet. Had she not started to get overenthusiastic, I would have really thought of her as a friend and an acquaintance, and would have been keen on keeping in touch. It was inexplicable to me when she and the young fellow working there started to treat me with less respect. I suppose they wanted me to stop working there on my own accord, as opposed to them sending me away. I suppose that was just after Nora's wedding.

I used to be fascinated by Vera's stories about Moscow, as much as my Columbian colleague Nora, who would talk about Bogota and Medellin. They were now ruled by the drug lords and were in the news every day, those beautiful places that she had grown up in. She had worked in the shop selling emeralds to American tourists. The way that South Americans talked about the nature around them when they were growing up reminded me of India and Pakistan.

"Houses in the countryside"

The sea and the wilderness of the undeveloped land with lots of undiscovered beaches, and places still untouched by tourism, were full of wild people, with machine guns in their hands, rebelling against injustice by living in the forests. Nora's family were in the retail business, and she was already married and divorced. Now she was getting married a second time, to a Turkish man who was working in the shop next to us. That shop was a Turkish shop. Her husband happened to be blue eyed and blonde, and he had chosen to call himself with a Western Christian name.

There were some Arab men as well working in that shop. One was an attractive Egyptian called Mehran. I though Mehran really resembled the antique statues of the ancient Egyptians; he was really, truly one of the most beautiful people I have ever seen in my life, but he was modest about it. He was married to an Italian girl who worked as a guide in Egypt, but it was obvious that he was on his way to a divorce. I liked Mehran as a person. I was thinking of introducing him to my Algerian friend Nadia who was twenty four, and who had said that she wanted to get married to an Arab. But that wasn't to be.

Dialogues Series; "Just Obey!"
Watercolour 1987

It was funny how, on Nora's wedding day, I had gone into the loo at work and had cried my heart out. I was thirty-two, still a student and felt like a total loser, utterly alone and incapable of ever being able to find a suitable partner. But I wouldn't take any steps in the direction of working something out with the people around me, like Nora had done. I wouldn't go out to parties like Cristiana, and I wasn't trying at all to find a remedy to my ailment. I had tried to introduce my friend Mr X into my life, but it hadn't worked out at all. Even Cristiana had tried to give me a few tips about how to put the relationship in the right direction.

Later on, I realised that sentimental issues are really difficult. Mehran had found a Palestinian girl whose father had told him that his daughter was in love with him. Her father actually worked for this lucky girl, in order to make the connection. I thought it such a precious thing that one could have a friend like that. He put them on the path as it were, so Methad went on to get married a second time, and was happy with his new family.

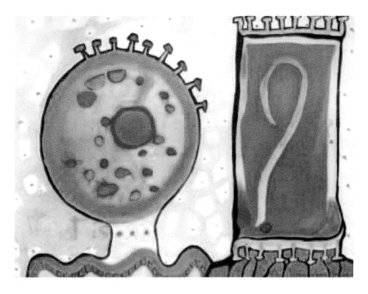

I was harbouring so many pressures in those years from personal and university life that when an Arab colleague from Yemen, a salesman from the shop next door, started to act as a watchdog on me, I thought him strange, but didn't take much notice of it. Just as much as I was aware of the microphones in the shop controlling us, I thought that they all went together with the fact that Mr C the shop owner was a declared fascist. He used to tell us about the time when, as a young boy, he would go to Piazza della Signoria in a black shirt and the Fascist salute to take part in the rallies during Mussolini's regime.

Mr C was sixty years old and had the wizened face and expression of a renaissance painting. He reminded me of a Gozzoli fresco in the Medici Palace. Like these people that had lived in these cities centuries ago, Mr C was wise and careful about what he said. He took his wife Veras naïveté in his stride. In a way, he had psychological insight into people's feelings.

Even though Mr C was a fatherly sort of figure, I felt that I couldn't very well go and complain to him about what had happened to me. My feelings of being molested in the shop were difficult to express. I thought people would have laughed it off and made the insult seem of no consequence. That's why I thought I would sue them and get money out of them, because it was the least I could do to defend myself.

When I told my Aunt Ylva, she said on the phone let bygones be bygones. But she hadn't felt the humiliation and suffering like I had. I thought that it would make them think twice about it before they made a pass at someone else at the work place. They might have thought that it had been a joke, but I didn't. I was determined in having justice, because my only fault had been to be a single woman with no one defending me. I had always dressed decently, covering up, as opposed to my colleague Nora, who had worn really short tops which were very fashionable, revealing her belly button.

On the last day of work at the shop, I had an appointment with Sharon and I had gone to the supermarket to buy biscuits. I found Mr C standing there as if he had something to say to me. Should I have lamented like a child and told him about Anja and Enrico's joke of touching me? I am sure that they also had CCTV in the jewellery store, so they probably saw what had happened and knew about it. It was a sort of practical joke. Later on, after some years, I saw a woman doing this to her young girlfriend in front of me, and I was appalled by the innocent girl's confused look.

'Heart of Glass' (from the film with the same name)

Mr C wasn't stupid; he knew that if I had talked to him, I probably would have let the whole unbearable thing go. But there was the shame that I felt about the whole thing, as if I had to put up with such nonsense in the work place. That is why I went to the lawyer's office.

In 1996, my American flat mate Eric Black came back to Florence and he came to visit me. I had painted the apartment blue, and for me it was the house of the ninety nine names of God, because I had written those names in all the rooms. It was a crazy time because I was living in my own world and far away from reality. Perhaps Sharon was trying to tell me this when she came to visit, and her words meant to tell me that. I should have taken it upon me to point out that it hadn't been nice of her to tell me off like that; that I was an artist and therefore not as capable as her to deal with the real life issues. Most probably, she couldn't fathom why I was sitting at home with a degree when I could have been working like she had done. I hadn't told her or anyone else about what had happened at work. I thought it was too embarrassing, and many people couldn't understand my point of view at all.

Eric took some pictures of the house, the paintings and the rooms, and even asked me to go to Germany with him. He had been to Berlin and that was after the wall fell in 1989. He was very enthusiastic about Berlin and the construction that was going on there. I was very tempted because I could understand Eric very well, we could have been good partners but I was on a certain path and I thought that I would continue on it. 1995 and 1996 were also the years of the war in Yugoslavia. The only person who was interested was Sharon, and I was grateful to have her and Nadia to talk to.

Some Jewish people wrote articles of protest against the rape concentration camps and the religious conflicts that were taking place there. Even Eric was politically aware of what was happening. The rape camps were places where Muslim and Croat women were impregnated forcefully by the Serbs in order to humiliate their opponents. I was glad that I painted two paintings with Sarajevo as the subject. However, after the war ended, it seemed pointless to paint political pictures because it was useless to protest.

Marco, who was a professional photographer, took the photographs of my paintings. He was practising Buddhism so he did it for free, but I gave him a painting in return. Marco was living a life very similar to mine. He stayed in his room and prayed. The Buddhists had a group and they met every week to pray together. We could hear them when they prayed together in his room.

He had a large room, which had a window looking on to the face of the Santo Spirito church. I was aware that the apartment he lived in must have been worth a lot, because of its position on the Piazza. It overlooked the whole square, and Marco had done rent control like myself. He made a living by renting out rooms. He was a homely type of person, you could tell, because he had very nice new Persian carpets in his room, and the place was always nice and clean. He would take care of his personal things, but he didn't care what would happen in the rest of the house. Eventually he bought himself a computer and started to work at home on his artistic photographs.

Mr X and Myself – Tizano and Sharon

I had met Mr X in 1989 or 1990, and even though he was just a young Iranian man from a simple background which was very working class, I preferred him to the Kurdish Mr Dariush, who had a degree in architecture and knew all the right things to say because he was a leftist. He was a cultured and educated type. I'd met them both at the Cultural Centre in Florence during the Iraq/Kuwait crisis. These two men symbolised the class division in Iran. On the one hand there were people in the majority who were uneducated or less educated belonging to the rural areas, and the working classes who were usually very pious and who supported the government and the revolution.

The other group of people were educated leftists and middle classes, who felt that they deserved privileges and that they were superior to the masses and the main population. Dariush represented the latter.

Dariush was very attractive and charming, but he was utterly and hopelessly self-centered, penniless and unemployed. He could quote Shakespeare and was an expert on cinema, but he was a man who wasn't earning – nor was I – and didn't have any prospects. Another point which wasn't in his favour was the fact that he was in a sort of close friendship with his Italian friend's American wife. Anyone could tell that she liked him a lot, so he was able to pick and choose.

One day, I went to visit him in the Cultural Centre, and he took me to the house of his American girlfriend. She was a soprano opera singer like my friend Sabina, and she sang in the Maggio Fiorentino. One could tell that she had put aside her husband and was really into Mr D. In fact, people have said since that they eventually married. I was astonished to see that this Italian man put up with their friendship going on right in front of him, between his wife and his best friend. I really felt sorry for him, but I thought that he must be a very generous man – or a cold-blooded, reasonable person – to be able to watch other people's happiness eat into his marriage. So even if Mr D asked me, I didn't accept.

Mr X was different. He was a pious praying kind of person who worked. He had managed to live a regular life and he pursued his interests, which were sports and cinema. I was awestruck by the fact that even though he was poor, he had managed to buy his parents an apartment. I think that is why I sort of respected him a lot. However, later on I found out that he had a woman in his life, although he said that he wasn't married. I didn't want to fall into having a husband who was already married. But by the age of thirty and thirty-one, everyone around me was with someone. There was a voice within me that said he wasn't good for me. I suppose I found out why when we went to Rimini with Tizano and Sharon.

Via Delle Cinque Giornate Apartment, 1995

I had been friends with Sharon since my degree party in 1992. We had common friends who had introduced us. Geoff and Matthew were people who were teachers of English at university and who were into theatre. I had known them for many years, since starting university. My degree party in Via delle Cinque Giornate was a big do, so they had invited their friends Sharon and Sara. They were all teachers of English. I really had a lot of respect for these people, as they were socially superior to me. I was an unemployed student and a renter of rooms. I had a lot of respect for Sharon and Sara because they were teaching, and even as language teachers they were following their artistic interests. Sara and Sharon were into singing and classical music and opera.

Pulsar
Watercolour, 1998

They were friends of Matthew to begin with, and I had spent an entire summer listening to Matthew complain about his Italian girlfriend M, who was already married. She was a wealthy lawyer and it seemed that there was no future in the relationship. Matthew's private life was well known to his friends – it was an 'event', and I suppose everybody watched his life with interest because he was an attractive man and with a very good sense of humour.

Geoff, too, was attractive, because he was the more middle class posh accent sort of person. Even though he wore a ponytail, you could tell he had a solid background. Geoff eventually got married and went to live in the States with his family. We were all dreaming of doing something big with our lives then. Matthew dreamt about being an actor and he defined art wistfully: "those sort of things that people who don't work seem to afford to do". Sharon too thought that teaching had its limits. Sara's attitude was more positive; she took teaching as a temporary situation, which was soon to change.

Serena and Elena and myself in the market at Santo Spirito, 1995

I liked Sharon and Sara immediately because they had a similar sense of humour. Matthew was very lighthearted, and when he was in the mood he could be very pleasant to be with. He was well liked because he was sociable and ready to mingle.

In 1992, when I met Sharon, she was just about to separate from her husband who she had been married to for some years. They had renovated an old house together and had fallen out of love when they had finished the job. Some people say that it is not good to renovate old houses with your spouse because of the pressure it puts on the relationship. But marriages and relationships were falling apart with many couples we knew, regardless of whether they were working on a project together or not.

Sharon revealed herself to be a woman who was very capable of starting a new life at thirty. She wasn't at all the sweet and simple type, and most Italian men usually like their women to at least pretend be one step behind them, rather than boasting to be running in front of them. I could see that she was feeling stifled in a women's traditional role in her marriage and she had already made the decision. When she got her divorce, Titziano had come into Sharon's life as a consequence of her wanting to replace her husband. Titziano was a very attractive Italian, thirty years old, from the outback of Prato. He looked just like the famous actor Nani Moretti. He was also someone who really liked cinema and intellectual things.

Sharon was just out of divorce and she was sharing her experiences with me and Sara, talking about her research for a new man, and Titziano sounded very good. Even if in the process of finding him, she had broken a heart or two.

Tizy, as me and Sara called him, was tall, dark and handsome, and had swept Sharon off her feet. He took her on sightseeing trips, things which she hadn't done in all her years of marriage. He was a bit too good to be true! She was very flattered to have found a sensitive man, who was also alive and had an interest in the world around him. He wasn't boring and he had made it clear to her, that he wanted to be the only one in her life. That was a pretty committing type of statement for someone to make just after her divorce.

Mr X was very sweet and had a sincere heart, but he thought that he still had time and could shop around. I was dating him because I wanted to get married. He was sensitive and smart, but didn't have the Italian leftist education that most educated or even uneducated people share in Europe. The jargon about cinema and any other art form is usually leftist in fact. Being an intellectual in itself belongs to the left. Only business people seemed to lean to the right. So Mr X didn't fall in place with these educated friends of mine, who were surprised about my choice.

After many years of living alone, I'd settled for someone so far from myself. People could tell that he wasn't the right sort of person. On one occasion at a friend's dinner party hosted by M, her friend, who was a Romanian and had lived many years in Germany, a very cultured man in his 1950s, started to say very unpleasant words which seemed to be directed at Mr X. Then again, before our trip to Rimini I could sense that people were not really accepting this person, and were putting up with him only for my sake. It seemed that I was being tested to see if I could defend him.

Titziano called us, in a general way, 'babuini' – i.e. 'the Iranian Monkeys', criticising us because we were imitating Western ways. He said quite a few unpardonable things on that trip, which were hard for me to bear. I did jolt when I heard his comments on the Serbs being the good guys in the war that was going on in Bosnia. Me and Sharon had just written a letter about the plight of the women in the so called 'rape camps' installed by them. They were provocative comments, and suffice to say that if I had felt totally helpless and full of rage by the injustice and insolence of his comments. However I kept quiet on both occasions, only feeling cold and distant. It was really not worth my while to get angry.

Poor Mr X could not defend himself at all socially. He was a meek type who needed a mother. I felt frustrated that I couldn't have someone by my side who could be strong for me. I should have been strong enough or clever enough to respond to Titziano's insults. He had really got to me, and I was ashamed of myself, for not being able to defend anything or anyone, not even myself. Sharon didn't say anything either, as if she had taken it in her stride. But she did know, the enormity of these gestures and words. I realised what women had to put up with when they have a partner.

It was sometime after our trip to Rimini that Sharon came to my place one day. She said she was upset because Titziano had told her a terrible thing and had expected her to accept it as well. He had told her this thing about himself in a lighthearted manner, as if she would have to accept it if she wanted to have him in her life. Later on she quit seeing Titziano, as she couldn't agree with such an attitude.

Now I wonder if a dark force wasn't already operating in those years as well, putting us to the test, as it were. Titziano was not at all unmanly in his ways. I was an idiot for telling Matthew what had happened between Titziano and Sharon. But Sharon hadn't told me to keep quiet about it. I mean, I was shocked myself and couldn't bear this burden of Sharon's words which weighed on me, and I felt confused. I was astonished to hear Matthew agree with Titziano. That was an extremely revealing conversation. I was like, "Am I the only person who can understand how Sharon must feel about this?"

That was in 1992, 1993 and 1994, and the war in Bosnia was raging. The war in Kuwait had brought me out of my room to meet people and I had met Mr X. He was more spiritual than anyone else I knew in Italy, except for Nadia. Nadia was living in the front room in Via delle Cinque Giornate. She was twenty three when she took the room, and she was a very reserved young lady. She had been born and brought up in the north of France, but her family was from near Algiers. It was fascinating because she brought a totally new experience and point of view into my life. She didn't know any Arabic, not even enough to read the Holy Koran. However, she said her prayers and tried her best to be Islamic.

We had many conversations about the state of things in the Muslim countries, especially since in those years a strange phenomenon was happening in the Algerian countryside, whereby villages and their inhabitants where being attacked and burnt by ruthless mercenaries who were absurdly called Muslims by the media.

We were both sure that such strange things could not be perpetrated by Muslims, since in the news they said that the new non-religious government was not allowing the inhabitants to have guns to protect themselves, nor was it doing the job of protecting itself. Furthermore a free general election resulting in the people's choice of an Islamic tending government was inexplicitly cancelled. Why was this happening? I remember once we were walking in Via della Pergola and we were talking about this situation and she was hysterically asking if this was Islam that was practiced in her country, "is this Islam?" I was trying to explain to her that at times the people who actually did the horrible things blamed everyone else and got away with it. It was really a well-known strategy.

About the same time, there was an article in the papers about a young mercenary who had been captured after such terrible acts, and he confessed that he had done all sorts of things under the effect of drugs, and was not aware of what he had done afterwards. Which made sense. Much more than Islamic militants killing innocent locals, it was the greedy people who wanted the villages to themselves who had paid him, he said. This article was in the Italian papers.

Nadia stayed at home and locked in her room most of the time, reading and learning languages, while she was looking for a job. She was a practicing Muslim, even if modern, and she didn't want to get involved with anyone. She was even wary of me and treated everyone who wasn't her family as "a stranger" and not to be trusted.

In one respect, she was right. It seemed that one took a risk every time one trusted a friendship because loyalties were very fragile, to say the least. She was right in staying in her room all the time and trying to work out what she had to do next. I realised that she was trying very hard to get a grip onto her life. I suppose she was realistic in not dating anyone, because even though she was an attractive twenty something, she knew that finding the right partner was an arduous task.

Sharon was very disappointed in me for having talked to Matthew about her private life and her experience with Titziano. She looked at me with new eyes, as if I couldn't be trusted. She did not realise that I was as shocked that she had confided such a delicate matter to me in the first place. She had put a burden on me which was too much for me. I really felt things deeply, and I felt sympathetic to what she had gone through. And she hadn't told me to keep quiet about it.

Later on, when I met Hans, the blonde Danish boy at Sara's door in Piazza Santo Spirito, I wasn't thinking of Sharon at all. Hans was being introduced to Florence in the Piazza by an Italian woman who said that he was looking to rent a room. I was always on the lookout for renters, and since I had just finished my thesis, I needed to rent the rooms again. Hans was not a very pleasant person, especially when he said something about me prostituting my rooms when I showed him the room. This was very impolite, to say the least. I had known another Hans from Denmark who had been a Catholic and a very special person. Therefore, I thought this Hans would be okay, since I had had a positive experience with northern people in general. Hans turned out to be educated. He was a computer person and had a degree in engineering, but liked to introduce himself as a blacksmith. Why did I ever think of putting Sharon and Hans together? God only knows.

Had I been a calculating woman with my head screwed on the right way, I would have cultivated this bachelor even for getting myself a European residence – something which Sharon had done – and would have tried to get rid of my Iranian passport. It was always a problem for visas and stay permits. Any red-blooded Iranian would have seen Hans as an opportunity not to be gifted to other women. However, Hans had uttered a dark series of words which made me feel wary of him. He had also told me that I would die by taking my own life, and that, was not sweet of him at all!

His being an educated man made me think that that was what Sharon needed in her life because she herself was into education and was bookish. I sound like a do-gooder and a matchmaker, but really I was sorry that a woman of Sharon's calibre should be wasting her time on people who were very much inferior to her, I thought it such a waste. I acted as a real Eastern friend, someone who cared. Nobody except Carina had cared for me; if I was alone and rotting away in solitude, it was my own fault entirely, but I was living up to the philosophy that had I acted positively, I would get the good energies back from the universe.

Hans wasn't charming at all in his manners, but I felt that he was a person who was worthy of being helped and that is why I introduced him to Leonardo, who was an IT consultant, and was looking for someone to help him. Later on I introduced him to Sharon and sent them off to the movies together – he had asked me, but I wasn't interested; I was still thinking along other lines.

I was actually surprised pleasantly by Hans some weeks later when he commented on how some people in town used bad language in relation to the Prophet Jesus (may peace be upon him) and the Virgin Mary. He thought it was a scandal to hear such insulting language and had stood up in one conversation and had left the room, saying that he would not tolerate such things. In fact it was surprising to find some people saying that they didn't believe in any of the biblical stories and that these two revered names had been ordinary people, under the rule of the Romans. Such people believed in the power of the secular society and its rules more than anything else.

I had a new respect for Hans after that, and I was grateful that someone had stood up for the revered Prophet and the Virgin Mary, because in Islam we feel a great deal of reverence for them, and it is a great sin to speak of them as normal, ordinary people. For Hans, behaviour in this matter I felt that he had well deserved my help and friendship. My having introduced Sharon to him was good too. Later on I fell out with Sharon for having done that. She came back from a holiday in New York to visit me, and during our relaxed conversation she had suddenly become very stern and had told me to "grow up"; however she had said it in a way which couldn't be pinned down. I couldn't accuse her of having said this to me and ask her to explain.

She had been totally weird, as if talking to a wall and not a well-wishing friend and I thought to myself, "naturally! My doing good was not appreciated at all." I wasn't competing with anyone over anything and yet here I was being sat upon in my own kitchen by this woman. I suppose I had foreseen this and I was not going to be unpleasant and fight, but I let it go and I thought, "good luck to you, you obviously don't need me in your life anymore."

Later on, I thought that it was probably a different point of view on life in general which separated us. I noticed a lot of people were uttering absolutely absurd things and getting away with doing so; it was as if they would somehow get promoted for saying the most horrible things and uttering the biggest lies, and I was wondering why this was happening. Then I read somewhere that it had something to do with Stalin. Or was it to do with Europe? A new era had begun,

All religions and philosophies talk about the concept of "caring for each other" – "treat others as you would like others to treat you". We are here to care about each other/ I mean, people read books but do they think about values? Human feelings, all the good things of the heart belong to the religious minded and if we don't live up to the rules of God, who will? No materialist gives away the things that they need themselves.

Since my biggest dream had been to live in New York, I was very happy when Sharon called me from New York where she had gone for the holidays. But when she came back, she was pretty hard on me and told me to "grow up".

We were sitting in the kitchen in Via delle Cinque Giornate and she was just back from her trip. I was being very wishy-washy, talking about Eric and Sara and how it was going for them, whilst I knew that Sharon and Hans were now together. In a sense, I was in a weak position because I didn't have anyone in my life again. I had given up on Mr X. My first reaction to Sharon's intellectual somersault when she criticised me was that I was totally dumbfounded. I couldn't believe that she could be harsh and unkind to me after my being thoughtful about her. I mean, no one was introducing me to a nice young man, but I was being generous to her life as a whole. I mean I know the worth of what I had done for her, because I so much needed a partner in my life myself. And this woman had the gumption to come to my house and tell me to grow up! How ungrateful can one get? I got the feeling that she was thinking, "You are such a loser! You haven't got anything going for you". Was that an acceptable attitude? Today I compare that to Mr Sedley's fate in *Vanity Fair*, where he says, "Some people don't like to be reminded that they have been helped". I didn't even expect a thank you, but I expected her to understand the positive thoughtfulness that I'd had for her and to take it into account.

I suppose the tide of the concentration camp attitudes or Zionist jig of heartlessness had already been there for a long time and that I was experiencing it for the first time. Good luck to you, I thought. But that's all the time of the day that I can give you.

- The Zionist jig is a condition whereby a good relationship is blown away by actively sowing the seeds of hate rather than love.

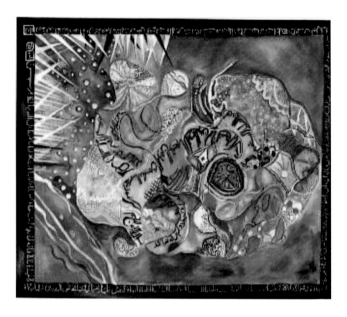

'Existence'

'Existence' was sold to a Danish couple in 2008 by Roberto. I am worried about these fascists having my paintings at all. Especially this one, which has always meant so much to me.

This is another painting that I started at one corner and didn't know about the outcome.

It is a violent one, with the soft cell amoeba in the middle and the needle-like things representing life's difficulties for all creatures in order to survive in the blue earth and oceans which we are living in.

The amoeba is a living unit, and in it there is the writing of Surat al Hamd, the first Sure in the Koran. Because as a living unit, me being the amoeba, I had this written in me when I started out. But the needles promise a difficult time. One of the unexpected geographical twists and turns, ups and downs, where a voyager finds that in the next corner and angle of a street a block of houses or a mountain or a valley, there is something unforeseen waiting for us little creatures. Even though the amoeba is fairly big – however, it is totally vulnerable and flexible – it tries to roll over things, bumping into or bouncing over all needles. It tries to survive by being adaptable to any shape. That is why the soft cell can survive.

I was working on the images 'Existenz', 'Da-sein', 'Being There', and 'The Invisible Pillars', and I thought that my life as a woman at thirty or thirty two years of age, was never going to work out. I was living in the front room in Via delle Cinque Giornate. Nadia had been living in the room next door to mine. Then there was Verena in the room at the back. Nadia and Verena were in my life when I started to do these images, as was Mr X.

I asked Mr X, why don't we get married? I suppose Mr X had problems in his life. He said in the beginning that he didn't want to ruin my life! I suppose he was a good guy, and now I understand what he was saying. I had gone looking for him that August of 1990 or thereabouts, and he wasn't there. He said he'd been to Austria for a week's holiday. I could tell that he was pretty self-centred and that he wasn't that much into me. I suppose that I wasn't that much into him either; he was just my nostalgia for my family and the past.

That was existence. I thought I wanted to go back to where my roots are, I wanted to seek my identity in him and his little world. He was so organised in his little world, and I admired that so much. I admired the fact that he'd sent money to his parents and they had bought a house with the savings that he had sent them. Such dedication was sort of Japanese – very loyal and very sincere, and I respected this young softly spoken man, even though I felt that he really wasn't up to the mark. I mean, even physically, he was a weakling and very cold, I thought. But, the fact was that he wasn't that much into the relationship because he had another woman, who wasn't going to let him go easily.

Such emotional strain made me believe that men were all double crossing shits, and one couldn't really expect any better. Because, I suppose, I was the unlucky girl who couldn't find a partner. Philippe was the one who was so out of reach, and he had actually asked me to get engaged! What was it that made me fly over the treasure that I so much desired? I went on thinking about Philippe for over a decade, following his shadow everywhere. I think that I was overawed or I wasn't up to the responsibility. I have never been one who listens to people anyway, and I never follow.

But I did follow Mr X, because he was the sort of man who prayed, and in a way he was humble, especially in front of his creator, and I thought that he was a good boy. Whereas with everyone else I knew that it would be a struggle, with him and I knew there would be peace. However, as life would have it, he had gone away on holiday without even thinking of telling me, which showed that he really couldn't care less. Such a typical situation. But my prophetic soul, I knew he wasn't good for me just the first few times when he expressed the opinion that "women were smelly", which was really offensive. His other opinions about women were downright sexist – a wife shouldn't get a chance to dominate or influence a man's opinion and ways of his life. Words that made my hair stand on end! So why did this guy follow me around when he knew that I was a free spirit? Looking back on it all now, I think that it was probably planned that way.

I thought about Francesca and her 'muratore'[16] (translates into construction worker) boyfriend. This guy was very good looking, one of those Florence people who have antique features. He had big doe-like eyes and seemed to be a sensible

---

[16] I am sorry that a worker's status still leaves a lot to be desired in Iran and some other middle eastern countries. Here workers (today) have no insurance or syndicates to protect them from whatever may happen to them at work and therefore their social status is very vulnerable and weak. The Iranian revolution didn't bring such workers the benefits which they deserved. I witnessed how a group of construction workers had to live in the building which was being built next to my house without proper heating facilities to protect them from the cold winter days and these same workers had to ask me the favour of supplying them with gas from my house. In another instance one young man who had gone through something serious at work and had been helped by a kind bystander while the person responsible had run away and left him to his own devices i.e. no insurance.) The respected status that a European worker enjoys in the west is 'still' the dream of many workers in the third world and the developing countries.

type of person. When she met him, they were always together and she wasn't alone, like she used to be. She even got him to study her English Literature books and got him to get a degree in English Literature. That was amazing, and it was refreshing to think that someone in this class-ridden world of ours could be different. Love could make a difference after all and a middle class girl could contribute to the uplifting of a boy from a working class.

So, why couldn't it happen with Mr X? I suppose, because he already had one forty year old middle class lady in his life, and didn't need another one just then.

That was one of the most difficult summers in my life, and I am glad that Verena was there for me. Verena was my sweet angel, and she was a true sister in the solidarity that she showed me, whereas Nadia, was probably judging me to be a loser. I guess it was pretty obvious which direction it was going to go and she was already onto the results of this – God's exam. She knew that these kinds of men couldn't be fair minded because she had several brothers herself. So she knew that I was going to have problems because some sexist men are not there and not friends of women. Usually they are antagonists and they can only at best be indifferent, but never sincere. Nadia was very neutral at that time, but I needed a real friend, and Guido called up and said why don't we get married and create a family? However, even though I needed him, I said no. This was because I couldn't forgive him for running off to the Philippines with Amor, the girl he'd got to know on the train. I couldn't trust him anymore. He had been lying through his teeth and wasting my precious years, and I was following him loyally, only because he was kinder to me than my own family. He did save me from a lot of things and I was grateful, but since he never listened to me, I thought it was useless. I suppose I was after a dream. Someone like my father, who listened to my mother and respected her ideas and opinions.

This was my existence in those years, and the images I was working on said these damned men are only a waste of time; why should I be running after them, when all they can do is to humiliate me and make me feel like shit? I felt like the Iranian women who worked on the carpets. That carpet creativity allowed the women to get away from the male dominations in their lives for at least a few hours. Ideally if there was respect and love and only respect and love, then perhaps we could have created a family. I wouldn't have been an amoeba anymore. I wouldn't be trying to catch hold of the moments and seconds so much. I suppose trying to catch hold of one's time and hours means that one wants to get control, have control over one's life and all the possible things that may happen. Had I been more easygoing and 'normal', I would have married Guido, even though, he didn't have a job and had children, and made myself a life with him in Italy. I owed him that because he had been good to me emotionally; he had the patience like a true friend to cure me when I was hurt, and nobody else had ever been that good to me saving me from madness. I suppose going to university and finishing that formal education saved me. But I think to myself that reading the Holy Koran would have had the same healing effect, and it would probably have brought me more barakat.

My existence got very complicated. A lot of the time we don't realise that other people are amoebas just as much as ourselves, trying to survive the world and our own life.

If I had been a cleverer woman, I would see that men too take a woman for the good things that she can add to his life. It was only years later that Serenella and Enzo came into my life, both Florentine people who had rationalised this process. As Serenella put it one day – she was good wife herself – she said that, "Enzo wants a woman who doesn't spend too much and who is companionable". The good things she can add to their life.

I like this painting very much because of the balance i find
in it. It is "just right". .... i was friends with Francesca & i
think that's where i got the poem from. One day i was at her
house & she started reading T.S Eliots poem for me ....
"The love Song" of J. Alfred Profrock".
which starts with: "Let us go then you & i
          when the evening is spread out against
          the sky ...."
& has this tired air of dragging ones drunken feet on the
pavement, then every once in a while it says:
  in the room the women come & go, talking of michelangelo

Paintings, 1984-2010

Italy Via delle Cinque Giornate
Oil Paintings, 1984-1998

The Contact of Aliens with Humans

1. The Contact

This painting, 'The Contact', was sold in Dubai in the winter of 2008-09, by Roberto in a Dubai gallery called Mondo Arte. R is a thirty year old artist himself, and he had had a feeling for this picture when he first saw it. Later on he stretched the canvas and put it up on show, together with the rest of the paintings I'd shipped from Italy.

'The Contact' was done spontaneously. I mean, I hadn't a clue about what I was doing or where I was going. It just happened. However, I must say that I had seen this film – it was 'Independence Day'. Such a Star Wars type movie, always excited my imagination.

It made me express my belief that there was intelligence in the universe, but what I was really talking about was pretty earthly itself. I mean, it's a contact of relationships – i.e. it is about when you find someone who you can really relate to, someone who opens up the world to you from a totally different angle, and that becomes a phenomenon in itself, because through a real contact you can also see surreal things.

*This was written before the black Fukushima episode in March 2011.

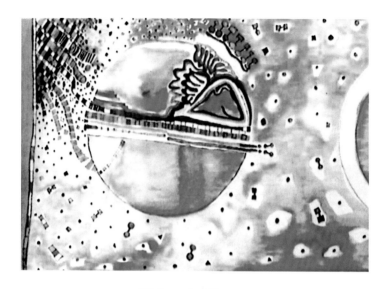

Vision of a Planet
Watercolour, 1990

I took this painting to Pakistan, thinking that the words from the Koran would make it interesting to someone from an Islamic culture. However, I had to take it back to Dubai because no one wanted it, even Auntie Jahan, who had wanted a big painting on her wall, and I had brought it especially for her. R said that an American client at the gallery had it now.

The Koranic writing says, "Do not the rejectors of the faith know that the galaxies and the earth were all one single mass and we blasted them apart? Then we caused rain to fall and give life to earth…We made every living thing out of water, will they not believe in Allah?" God the mastermind is taking credit for his creation.

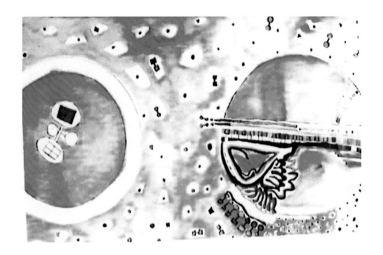

Vision of a molecule
Watercolour, 1990

I was overjoyed that it was sold. I don't think that my other big paintings will ever be sold now because, as is the situation in 2009, there is a general economic crisis and nobody seems to be spending money on such items.

So I got lucky that time. R left the gallery and the gallery closed down after some months. Actually, the story is that I got to know R through A, who worked in the gallery full time. She was very stressed by her new job, but she liked my work and accepted them in the gallery. Then I met R who I thought could be related to her – I was wrong. Later on, I realised that he must be very young – perhaps not even thirty.

Cosmopolitan Time painting in the blue apartment, 1995

When he took over responsibilities from A because she had an argument with the owner, he was just as stressed, but he was friendly and we talked about various things. He told me that he had gotten to know Raffaella, who was the directress in the gallery, whilst he was running a flower shop somewhere in the periphery of Milan. Raffaella had brought him to Dubai, and so he had been living in Dubai a few years.

Raffaella was a woman one never met at all. Behind the scenes somewhere being totally irresponsible. I say this because one of the 'slimies' had damaged one of my paintings in the gallery whilst A had been there. I saw this poor painting being mistreated, and Anna didn't do anything to fix or repair it, even if she said she would do it.

When R took over, he too didn't do anything about repairing it, even though he said he would. So finally, I repaired it myself, taking some instructions from this other painter called Paolo Maria. Paolo was friendly and interesting to talk to.

When I had finished repairing the painting with more gold leaf, and it had become a beauty, a couple from Denmark walked in and wanted to buy it. They took it without paying for it, and I was left with the choice of accepting the fact that I had very little power to protect myself and my interests if the gallery didn't do it, or to fight with everyone and leave, protesting the only way I could. I chose to let the painting go and say nothing – i.e. not make an issue of it. They were probably part of an elite group, I mean, the Danish couple, and I had had to be a victim of their privileged status.

The young client said that he had participated in the Bosnian war, so I suppose he enjoyed getting something for free.

Cosmopolitan Time
Oil on canvas

The young man who had worked for the UN in the Bosnia area was talking about the Sarajevo pictures and I thought it was my duty to participate in the sale of the painting. Our conversation was civil to begin with, but later on he said some unpleasant things and so did his young wife, and that was when I realised that they were out to get me. It was a power trip on their part. Later on R, who was totally taking their side, hence meaning to say, "go away from the gallery if you don't like what we are dishing out to you" in a silent slimy (means invisible mischief maker) fashion.

Sarajevo
Oil on canvas, 1995

I had been in a similar situation before and I had lost out and suffered. I chose to accept the situation, even though I had counted on the money because I needed it. R said afterwards, "We are living in a war situation" (2007). It was sincere, his speaking frankly. I thought, "thank you, R – you are a kind person after all", and even though this is rough on me, I'll bear with it. Time will sort this out. Being a Muslim and a woman on her own is not going to protect me. I'll have to do like the prophet Jesus Christ and try to rise up upon this and many other occasions.

'Time Warp'

This painting was sold by Mondo Arte gallery in Dubai.

I was listening to a program on the radio in Florence when there was a programme called 'Time Warp'. I like this painting a lot. In a black and white world, there is not much space for the greys.

'Time Warp' is about our psychological time; not the time that flows in the ticking clock, but the one which derives from our consciousness and experiences. That's why, for some people, time stops at a certain event or age, for others, time is a cycle which is always returning, whereas for others it goes in a straight line ahead. I'm thinking about how time is a flow of our personal feelings; a map with roads and lanes and landmarks.

Pulsar
Watercolour, 1989

The reason why I did cosmic paintings was because I've always been a starry eyed teenager, and I am really impressed with astronomers who search out the Milky Way and that sort of thing. I mean, I wish that had been me. I am sure that I would have been a different, better person if I were involved in astrophysics. However, I can only afford to dream and this painting just leaped out of my imagination.

The first one of such cosmic types was the one that I started to do in Pakistan whilst I was staying with my aunt in her house in Karachi. Her name is Jahan, which is such a big name, meaning 'the world' when translated from Persian. Could it be a coincidence that such big ideas were in my mind then? That watercolours were a rather 1960s type and sort of psychedelic, whereas 'The Contact' was an oil painting with a bit of gold leaf. It may be a metaphor for myself as an individual, so far away from people whilst in the midst of the crowd. That is how I have always felt. And now I think this 'Contact' business is really not about aliens, but about people who are alienated and finally find a relationship, which makes life worthwhile the living. I suppose some call it love with the big L.

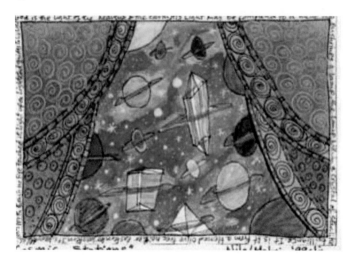

Cosmic Stations
Watercolour, 1999

I remember watching some movies with Sharon and Sara in 1993. I was so proud of being friends with Sharon who was socially in a higher league than me, being an English Language teacher at the university. We could talk about politics and ideas, rather than the day-to day things. I don't know if I saw this movie with her or not. But, she was a planet and we had made contact. For a while there had been communication and that was good.

The Koranic verse here translates into a rational view of the creation of the Universe, but in a personal sense the universal creation is also a sort of communication... by God to the individual. 'The Contact' is from Surat al Anbia v.30 and it says, "Do not the rejecters of faith know that the galaxies and the earth were all one single mass and we blasted them apart?" It gives me such deep emotion that here the creator is saying, "I did this". He takes possession of his role and says, "If you didn't realise this before, then I'm telling you NOW, I created the galaxies and I'm the mastermind of all that you know and don't know".

It continues: "Then we caused rain to fall and give life to earth...we made every living thing out of water; will they not believe in Allah?"

I interpret this line as a dialogue between God and man i.e., the individual {someone like the Prophet Abraham asks God the Mastermind: 'How did you create the universe?'

And God in his benevolence responds: 'I created the Universe and I did it like this'

It continues by explaining the process of creation:

God the supreme Architect and Engineer says: 'I created the universe... and I caused the rain to fall on earth so that living creatures could thrive'.

In a way we are being told that everything has a reason for which is exists in the process of creation and existence.

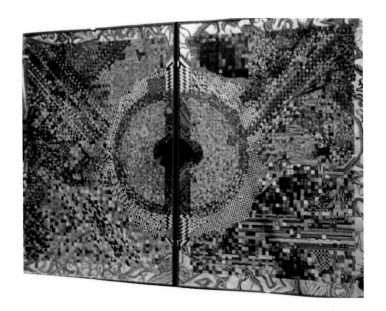

Back to the Centre
Watercolour, 1980

My deep belief and faith in the creator is expressed here in the painting. Perhaps in a moment of real inspiration and contact with the divine, I want to say, "I've been blessed and I have seen the light – in a mystical experience".

I have finally seen God the creator through his work.

3. Sarajevo

The Bosnian War was especially important to me because, as a Muslim who had lived in Europe for thirty years, I felt that the bridge that I believed in, was being rubbed out of history. The Arabs and the Islamic culture were totally made unacceptable.

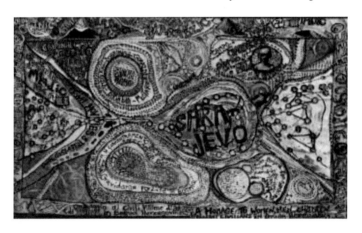

'The Painting Called Sarajevo'

Sharon was a teacher of English and the University. She was an assistant who had been working as a teacher for many years. She'd married an Italian, a Florentine electricity technician. Having renovated a house together, they were now at a stage where they were getting a divorce. I met her at this stage. She was a friend who came to Matthew's house.

In fact, I remember walking down the street in Via del Cerretani one evening and I heard my name being called by someone who was running behind me, rather desperately, to catch up with me. I was surprised and a bit flattered that anyone should do that for insignificant me. That's how I remember me and Sharon becoming friends. She had come to my graduation party at Via delle Cinque Giornate, together with Sara, Matthew and Jack. They also came to the exhibition I had at the women's library. It was Guido's last days with me and it was so unfair because he had been the one to help me through university and now I had this bunch of new friends.

Sharon was intellectually stimulating and we were both interested in politics and what was happening in Bosnia. Especially those concentration camps where Muslim women were taken and impregnated by Serbian men in order to hurt the Muslim pride in general.

It was a Karadich tactic of psychological warfare put to use in this war. The things we use to read in the papers were probably a fraction of what the real situation was.

What can one do about the superficial world of glossy magazines, writing about women's clothes and sexuality but not about such real things that were about women being treated as less than human?

Sarajevo was really a big issue for me, so I painted pictures about it. But later on I regretted doing that because it was pretty useless me doing that. I suppose it was a way of saying, "I was here and I saw this happen". As if a handful of Jews protesting against the Holocaust as it was happening, would make any difference.

Sharon joined me in writing this letter to the editors of these magazines, reminding them about what was happening to these women and asking them about their intentions with regards to giving their public some information about what was happening.

I suppose what is the real issue is that every one of us would like to live a life as far from problems as possible. Hadn't I and my family always avoided political subjects during the Shah's time? We only wanted to get on with our little lives. We, none of us took part in the revolution – we weren't leftist and we weren't religious. A lot of people just want to get on with their lives and solve their problems as best as they can, because after all, life is so short.

'A Letter from Sarajevo'

This Serbian man who I knew because he was into the cultural scene and liked to watch arty films like the rest of us – he was a sensitive soul who suffered for the political situation in the Balkans, and he was getting into a depressed state of mind which eventually made him psychologically ill. You saw him around town, drinking himself into oblivion. He was one of the ones who didn't survive in the game of the survival of the fittest... whoever survives, because that's reality.

From the Holy Koran
The Chapter Al Noor (meaning Light) v.35 , 36

"God is the light of the heavens and the earth, his light is like this: there is a niche, and in it a lamp, the lamp inside a glass, a glass like a glittering star, fuelled from a blessed olive tree from neither east or west, whose oil almost gives light even when no fire touches it – light upon light- God guides whoever he will to his light; God draws such comparisons for people; god has full knowledge of everything"

Michelangelo, Sandra and Stephan in Viareggio, 2004/2005

Marina and Sandra

In the fall of 1998 I moved to via fiesolana studio and my dream of working as an artisan had come true. One of my prayers was that I would be able to earn enough money by being self-employed as an artisan, so that I could keep my prayers and work at the same time. I met Susan through the exhibition I had had in August and she had told me about Sandra. I imagined that the connection between Susan and Sandra was in the days when they were in their 20's. They had shared the zeitgeist of the 60's. Sandra had rebelled against her wealthy conservative family rules and had married a Columbian architect who wasn't well off. She had married for love and had worked as a teacher in order to contribute to the household expenses. When I first met Sandra it was in the late 80's. She was living in via Dei Bardi in an apartment on the ground floor.

Buildings by the seaside – Oil Painting 2007

The rooms faced a garden full of tall trees. In the summer of 1998 Susan had told me about the place but I hadn't made the connection in my mind. I had met the same person Susan was talking about.

She was talking about the woman with the big house in Viareggio and the apartment in Florence. I had been looking for a room to take on rent in an apartment years ago, because the responsibilities of having to run an apartment and study had been too much. I had seen her adverts (Sandra) at the British institute library and had gone to see her place after calling her on the phone. I myself had been renting the rooms in my apartment for many years now. I wanted to change my life. Sandra had two grey cats who had a whole garden to live in, and I was wondering if I could take my cat to live with me. My pets Mooshie and her daughter were sharing my life and I could understand that Sandra would not approve of cats in her place. The problem with having pets is that other people usually don't want them around.

Watercolour 2003

There was a romantic wooden shed in the middle of the garden at Sandra's house in the middle of the trees. It was being rented out and it looked like a little house in a fairy book. For one minute I thought that I could even bring my pets with me, but it didn't seem very practical. I had been looking for a really normal home.

It had been pleasant chatting to Sandra in her dream home and I left her thinking that she was a special person. I didn't see her again for many years to come.

Susan's description of Sandra and her children didn't give me any clue as to who she was talking about. My house hunting had made me visit many homes. Susan to have had the same sort of problem.

People who don't have money to buy their own homes often know about other peoples' houses just because they need to have a roof over their head. Susan had found a place in the mountain community and I had stayed in my apartment for many years. It was always nice to live in the centre of town and marina happened to be my neighbour living in the next street. We had been neighbours since 1984 when we started university. She had a little car, a fiat and she was employed as a full time secretary. I had seen her drive that car for many years, in fact she had had it right at the start of our meeting, now she had become a very competent driver and it was fun to be in her car and driving to the unknown situation ahead of us.(In 2005 we went to visit Syliva in Viareggio)

The Underwater Seascape
Oil on canvas 2008

I had been told by Susan that I should call Sandra and ask her about her about work as an assistant in her viareggio house come bed and breakfast. Now I was going to Sandra's place together with marina, I was taking her along with me to meet Sandra; it was like a little adventure.

I remembered the first time I had invited marina to my apartment, she had come along with her friend Angela and I had wondered why she had had to bring someone along with her. Now I saw that going somewhere with a friend is always comforting, because one has morale support. Some of my friends that drove had told me that they didn't like driving on the motorway, but marina was chatting about everything under the sun as she drove and that made me believe in girl power. I was proud of being with her because she was always so together and cool headed and balanced about everything.

Seaside House – Mixed Media 1997

We enjoyed each other's company and we had so much to talk about. Later on when we had met Sandra and Lucilla I was also grateful that she had come with me. After via fiesolana I had moved into a first floor in the countryside around the city of Pietra Santa. It was a long walk away from the train station, and one could hear the trains going on the hour. I had rented it because of the garden and because my pets could wonder about. I had taken marina to see this country house because since she'd known me, I had been living in Florence and now I was out of the city and living by the seaside.

1   Lucilla and myself
2   In the garden
3   The cook and Sandra's mother

It had been predictable that I would leave Florence because I wasn't really upwardly mobile. I hadn't found a steady job, Guido had left me and gone off with a Philippine girl called Amor and all I had left was my pretensions to art.

Marina had picked up studying for her university degree at 25, just like myself. She had come back to Italy from Germany where she had worked as a secretary in a well-paid job. She had decided to come back to Italy after having grown up into the German school system and she had a clear-sighted view and a plan about the things she wanted. She never talked about these out loud, but her passion and perseverance at keeping a job and studying for a University degree at the same time, were really admirable. She never complained about how hard it was to get through the day and always had time for everybody.

Cruising In The Countryside – Watercolour 2001

Her brother Antonio was in the police force and she would talk about his different girlfriends because he was an eligible bachelor. They had bought a house in the suburbs of Florence, he was staying at the ground floor and she was staying on the first floor.

Marina was practical and down to earth and I don't know how she managed not to harden up into a tough career girl, with all the things she managed to do. She never got out of being a nice family girl and a loving sister and daughter.

1 Teresa preparing the table
2 View of the back garden
3 Sandra, her mother and the cook

That Sunday in autumn the sun was shining down on us, it was 11.o.clock in the morning and a pretty chilly day. The place id rented in the countryside wasn't very promising at all. There had been strange going-ons at night and the cats were behaving very much out of character. I suppose the owners who lived on the first floor thought I wasn't very normal myself. From their point of view I was a foreigner who had bought in cats with her and a middle aged woman on her own.

Marina instead had her brother and fiancée around her, she seemed to be well protected and well adjusted. She was amused by my eccentricity I suppose that was why she still kept in touch. We looked into my place in the country and later headed out to Sandra's place by the seaside.

Swimming With The Dolphins – Oil painting 1988

The villa was just a little walking distance from the beach, you only needed to cross the road to get there. I found out later that the views from the window were magnificent and exciting, because the waves were rolling right in front of you.

We got to Sandra's place about noon when the sun had warmed up the front hall by pouring in through the large

French windows. Sandra and Lucilla were there to receive us. Marina was a great conversationalist and I found out that there was so much that I'd never known about her. The interaction between these 3 Italian women was interesting because they had all such a rich amount of memories, experiences and tenacity, which was much different from what I had found in other people.

**View of the piazza signoria from the window
Watercolour 2003**

Marina was Pugliese and from manfredonia the area where Padre Pio had spent most his life. All catholics have great faith and respect for this saintly man. His life and works especially his stigmata's were extraordinary and his life was impressive. Marina and Sandra, who were both believing Catholics, were talking about Padre Pio.

Sandra was speaking a lot about different things, which showed she was well read and interested in the world. I was meeting Lucilla for the first time in my life and the thing that was extraordinary about her was her simplicity and intelligence in speech, she was in her twenties and was about to drop out of university because she had to work for a living.

She was waitressing. She hadn't been able to finish university because it was impossible to study and work at the same time. It requires a lot of concentration to focus on books and exams. I could relate to what she was going through. Lucilla had gone through various exams but now seemed confused about what she wanted out of life.

One losses strength, when there isn't enough support from family and friends, I knew all about that sort of thing and I felt sympathetic. She seemed not to have anyone who encouraged her to get a degree.

It seemed such a miracle that I managed to pull through University after all those years, what with the Iran Iraq war and little funds from home, I felt I knew very well how hard it was for her to study and work at the same time. Especially with a humanities degree, much of the courses at the university were for people who had time and money to continue studying. Journalism or teaching, were only possible after you had spent some years at private schools. I had seen my wealthier colleagues do that. They were the ones that then went on to professions.

In The Library – Oil Painting 2007

Momenti Brillanti
Oil on canvas 1990

I got lucky because even though I was very confused about how a thesis was written I had been introduced to Patrizia by an Australian professor at uni, and she helped me by lending me her computer and by giving me good advice. Incredibly enough just as I handed in my thesis the university fees for the next bunch of graduates went from a few 100,000 old lire to a million old lire. It would have been impossible for me to pay another session at uni never mind this incredible high amount.

As Lucilla was talking about her own experience, I knew perfectly well that for a woman her age the costs were an obstacle. I had known other people who had been passionate about getting through their studies.

Such people had no time for niceties and pretences and Lucilla was one of those people. She was a typical Italian girl jet-black hair and dark features were set upon very white skin and she had a striking beauty spot on her chin under her lips. She was what they called a truly archaic woman because she was really pretty and she grew on you.

We had talked about so many things the 4 of us it was astonishing to find that the hours had flown by and we had hardly said all that we wanted to say. I realised that after many years of solitude I was back in a world where there were people who were interesting. I loved Sandra's house, which reminded me of a similar place in Karachi.

The Sitting Room – Watercolour 2006

Seven bricks it was called and was owned by mother's second cousins a big old house where some generations had lived, memories filling up each and every corner. I felt that there was the spirit of the house by the sea, which would be positive. We had been sitting in a huge hall with very high ceilings over 4 metres with very tall windows with lots of light pouring in, the autumn skies were darkening as we left the place.

This front hall was probably the place where lots of people had had their romantic meetings, in fact I found out later that the buildings had been a hotel in the 20s and 30s and that Sandra mother had lived there all her married life.

Casa a Pietra Santa
Watercolour 2003

Later on, this ninety year old lady told us stories about her life in viareggio whilst we were sitting around the dinner table, especially episodes that had happened during the second world war. One of the stories was about how she had to pass through a checkpoint where the German soldiers checked everyone who was entering Florence. She had her very blonde blue-eyed baby son who they thought was a German boy because he looked especially different and that is why she got through the checkpoint. They had asked her if his father was German and she had playfully said yes just to get through.

The moral of this story she said, was that one had to go with the situation!

I sat with the old lady when Lucilla couldn't sit with her and looked after her at times but my stay at the villa began on a Sunday. I had gone out to look for a place to rent closer to Viareggio.

I was staying at Pietra Santa but it was cold and inhospitable. I felt that there were people there who were watching me closely.

Buildings by the seaside (triptic)
Oil on canvas 2008

In a sense Eric, Sara's boyfriend was right about Pietra Santa. It was a place for rich artists and if you didn't do sculptures, people couldn't really accept you. Maybe I was just too old and I couldn't pretend to be an aspiring artist anymore. I still sold my cards in a shop on the main piazza in the city but I found it difficult to get into the life.

Once I saw some very handsome Senegalese people, men and women in their national costumes coming in and out of a house just next to the main piazza. They seemed to be very happy and I was surprised that they didn't have any problems being black in an area that was very conservative.

Houses in the country
Oil on canvas 2008

Eric had such a lot of good things to say about Pietra Santa because he was a rich American type. He probably didn't get followed or watched at all. I was used to having this phenomenon in my life ever since I had moved to via fiesolana. Something was going on. Anna the gallerist in Borgo Pinti said that a lot of different groups of people were observing me even though I wasn't political at all.

I had come out of Pietra Santa thinking that I would speak to Sandra and see what she would say about me joining her staff for the winter. I knew that she preferred to keep South American people because she knew them well and they were flexible and good tempered. I had been followed by a group of people all that day. I had been walking down the beach road trying to phone up housing agencies and asking them about cheap rent for the winter.

The Kitchen
Oil on canvas 2008

Sandra, wasn't to be seen anywhere and as I waited there behind the big front window I watched Michelangelo Sandra's son. He was wearing a black jumper and pants sitting on the sofa with an afro American girl deep in conversation. I hadn't seen Michelangelo but I had heard his name mentioned a lot. You could tell that he had South American genes because he looked the type. He had a lot of dark thick black hair falling across his forehead and his features were peaceful. Their conversation made me think that he was a smooth and sophisticated type of person.

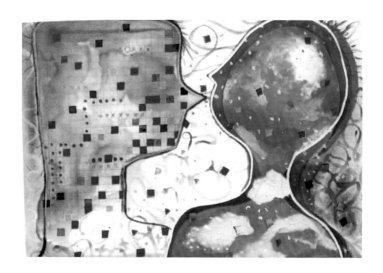

Dialogue No. 1
Watercolour 1992

However my first impression of Michelangelo would prove to be very wrong because, he had had many things which had darkened his life and he was far from being at peace with himself and the world. I would come to know these peoples stories later on and the reality would unfold itself but in this magic moment he would seem a "normal" man sitting with a "normal" girl; i.e. people who had no problems where as I was the one outside the door knocking and asking if I could be taken in for the night.

It was very hard to ask for Sandra's help but as I knocked and introduced myself, they called her to come to the door. She had been in the kitchen and came to greet me much surprised because we had only met once and now, I was introducing myself as her friend. I asked her straight if I could stay the night or did I even ask? That I can't remember because she led me away to a room upstairs and put me up for the night without a question or a word.

Later on, she sent her young Chilean assistant Carlos with some food up to my room. I couldn't believe it. This was a moment of need and I was very grateful to have found refuge in a safe place.

The Refuge
Mixed media 1987

I wished that I could have done the same for other people but I don't think that I would ever have the strength or the faith to do so. It was a relief to have solved my bed situation for the night and I went out again after dinner to buy a toothbrush hoping that I would find a pharmacy open in the area. Of course it was useless to think that anything else but bars and nightclubs would be open on a Sunday evening.

Next morning I woke up to the lively cries of the ducks and geese on the riverbanks next to the house, I had always noticed them on my walks but on this particular morning I woke up to hear them sing; it was as if they sang the praise to the creator.

It was a bright fresh morning to me because I had received this kindness from a friendly soul and the beauty of the place made life worth the living. There were rooms, which Sandra showed me later, which had windows that opened right over the sea. Breath taking views to wake up with, it made all the difference.

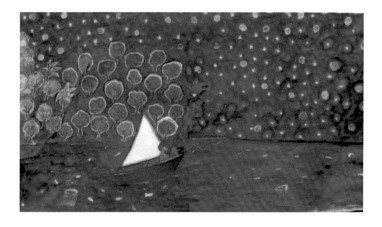

Boat out on the sea on a windy night
Watercolour collage 2008

Even though the building itself needed to be repaired it was still a grand old place. Its majestic marble staircase leading up to the first floor was really spectacular but the front halls that received the sun made it a happy joyful and a unique place.

However you realise it isn't the place that is the most important thing, it is the spirit of the people and how good they are that matters most. I had left Via Fiesolana city bustle and I was grateful for that. I had moved on with much difficulty and now again I was looking for my future in viareggio. My mother and brother had given me hopes that they would have liked to buy property in and around Florence but they never got around to actually doing it. They held the purse strings and they weren't really bothered by my problems abroad.

The Old City
Watercolour 2002

They were thinking that they wouldn't mind me going back to live in Tehran with them. They had dropped the idea of buying a place and didn't want me to stay on. My father however thought that I should settle down in the adopted country after having lived there for so many years.

I have reached the conclusion that if that one doesn't innovate then life itself makes the necessary changes for you. One has to make an effort to make positive changes, beneficial ones and all this requires courage to begin with, strength to continue the task and purpose to bring it all together. That is the ideal, however I didn't do too well in bringing it all together at all. I am sure that the only reason they were not making any more moves towards buying a place was because of fear. The fear of the unknown

The Metropolis
Watercolour Collage 2008

Sandra's way of life made me question my own decisions. I think, it was the Christian morality of giving hospitality that played a part in her accepting to take me on in her household. It was now winter and I needed a place because I couldn't pay more rent where I was staying. I called Lucilla and had invited her to come to my place in Pietra Santa. I was thinking that perhaps I could do some waitressing like she did or some other work in order to earn money. But my heart was in the white villa on the beach and I asked Lucilla to ask Sandra if I could stay with them at her house. There was no heating in the rooms upstairs in the winter months. So eventually, I went to stay where everyone else was staying and my pets stayed downstairs in the garden. Lucilla, Stephan and Teresa had rooms as well and I was given a room next to them. My stay at the villa began in the autumn of 2004.

The bedroom view
Watercolour 2008

Sandra ran the place as if it was her own family or community of people and certain rituals like dinner had been set. That was when people gathered around the big dining table next to the kitchen. Mrs Barini Sandra's mother who was 94 years old stood in the kitchen and helped the cook make dinner for people. Actually one of the girls had the set task of preparing the meal for everybody but grandma did help out on the kitchen in whatever way she could. She worked as an assistant cook, Sandra thought that by keeping her mother occupied, the old lady would get some exercise and lead a healthier life and she enjoyed being around other people,

I had been given the task of watering plants but after having done that I didn't know what to do so I did nothing and went for walks on the beach. No one in the house seemed to enjoy the beach. I found that these walks were a treasure which I had missed out on for many years. Living in Florence, wasn't like living away from nature because the countryside was only minutes away. But one got tangled up in the everyday chores and didn't make the effort of going out and seeking nature. Now I had the possibility to be with the sea breezes and the fresh air and the sound of the waves. I felt guilty about the times I had spent watching TV and I pitied my parents and people like them who had the TV on all the time. I am sure that they spent half their life in front of the telly like that.

The Sitting Room
Oil on canvas 2008

That is the way a lot of people live today in the world. It has probably something to do with enjoying a passive state of mind, you just let go and accept whatever is given to you without any effort.

Nobody in the white villa watched TV that much, but people stayed indoors a lot. Even on the very best days they couldn't be persuaded to go out for a walk on the spur of the moment. I think that everyone worried a lot, thinking their lives and problems wouldn't work out.

The Studio – 1998

However worrying and anxiety never makes things better. I had stayed cooped up in the room of my apartment for years because I had to get through exams and university, and once that was done it was the same happening again in via Fiesolana because I had to make a living. I had spent so much of my life in doors that I almost felt a guilty pleasure when I did go out for walks (as if it was a privilege that I enjoyed without permission from the adults!).

It's funny how one feels that one doesn't deserve to be happy and it follows that you want to give yourself a hard time just to fit in and please everybody else.

The Studio Entrance

In fact in the moment of happiness there is a thought that ups itself and says, what about all the unhappiness of humanity (just looking at the daily newspaper is enough to participate in all the known problems and ignore the ones that we don't know about).

We are always trying to control life but one way or the other sooner or later we find out that one can only make an effort in the right direction and hope for the best.

The Rough Seas – Acrylic on Canvas 1985

Like a small boat on the ocean we try to find the shore and if we are lucky, and God willing, we may find the island of happiness.

Happiness was what a lot of people were after, and one of these was Sandra's son Michelangelo. He said often that he didn't want to suffer, he wanted to be normal like everybody else but he hadn't found himself yet.

Metropolis
Watercolour collage 2008

When I met Michelangelo he was 35 years old; he reminded me of a darker shade of a young Roman Polanski, but he wasn't an ambitious boy at all. He had lost his way on his way to school when he was 16 and had been trying to come back home ever since.

I was working as his nurse/companion during that Christmas of 2004/05 because his girlfriend had gone home to Mexico. He was lost without someone to take care of him and I knew that I couldn't replace her warmth and affection. They sat next to each other like two kittens, the body language said we just want to be hanging out together.

The Computer Room – Oil Painting 2007

She wasn't a pretty woman, but she seemed caring and he was a vulnerable young man who needed to lean on a companion. Rosa Elena was her name and she had a laptop and was managing to swim with the tide while Michelangelo was struggling to keep afloat. He had stepped into the parlour of the "dealer" when he was a teenager in order to feel grown up.

He had talked about himself over lunch one day saying that when the dealers approached him he had felt powerful, as if he had found his place in society; becoming a man amongst men. Later on though when he was into the game, he had been frightened; but then it had been too late to turn back. I was wondering why I had never been attracted to drugs myself. I had been curious about them, and I had even read Aldous Huxleys book about tripping experiences but I didn't really feel that I wanted to have them in my life.

The Confused Couple – Oil on canvas 2008

When after years of struggle I came back home to my parents, my mother asked me "why didn't you become a drug addict like everyone else?" as if it was the only thing one could bring back home form the big wide world. I was astounded by the low opinion she had of me. All my life I had tried to get an education and aspired towards creativity and self-expression. Those highbrow things that can frustrate a young person and make you think that you will never make anything out of your life. I think what seriously saved me from falling into depression well and truly were my pets Mooshie and Mooshina who were nature's examples of how fun life can be once you have a roof over your head and enough to eat. They taught me how to be contented with little and to find a lot of love and joy in their playful company.

Mooshi and Mooshina 1984 to 2001

As far as work was concerned, Sandra had told me to water the plants but it didn't make sense to water them through the winter I did clean the rooms downstairs and chores like cutting the wood, or bringing in the washing.

At dinner we used to sit around the big dinner table beside the kitchen. Sandra liked everybody in the house to be sitting around the big table at dinner. D the cook was the one who looked after Sandra's mother in those months and she took her out for walks to the coffee shop during the day. It's funny how I had seen a man walking outside the villa the first night I stayed there and he seemed to be a living copy of this girl in his features only that he was taller. This stranger had looked at me in an inexplicable way as if to say, "you got in after all our efforts to make you desist"!

The kitchen table
Water colour 2009

The good food which old Mrs Barini and the cook made, went to waste because of the hot tempers of the recipients. Almost immediately the dinner table talks proved to be stressful and aggressive. Tension came from unexpected parts! I never imagined such problems at the dining table. I felt it was so unnecessary to be unpleasant in a gorgeous house like that which came with a hospitable Sandra as the owner. However people are so full of anxiety as a rule that if there is no control through rational thought they can easily become unbearable and mean in the most beautiful and comfortable situations.

D the cook kept her mouth shut and worked hard most of the time. She was a nice girl, into sports and I thought of her to be so distant from me in every way. She was on good terms with all the other young people and wouldn't get involved in the politics of the house.

The Mermaids
Watercolour 2007

Stephan was Sandra's best friend and much cherished by her during those days, because even though he had been involved in drugs he was coming out of it through his own efforts. Sandra paid him a lot of attention, somehow it felt as if she was trying to help Stephan in order to make amends for what had happened to her own son.

Michelangelo was not at all well. He was so unlike the man I saw that night sitting with Louise. I came to know that Louise was his American friend. She had been through the same problem but had somehow come through. But Michelangelo was pretty far-gone, deteriorated. I felt for him because he was very silent as if he had gone through a lot of hardship and no one else could help him anymore. He told me that his right arm was not working at all because of some accident which had happened some years ago.

But, Sandra used to hope that her boy would take up a job as a driver someday, driving with only one hand. She expressed those ideas once and I thought how extraordinary, she thinks that men are good for driving cars and that is what most of them do for a living now a days! Why hadn't I thought of that?

The Rainbow
Oil painting 1995

My own brother had driven a van around LA when he had lived there for some years. Somehow what was wrong with Michelangelo was something of a heart issue (I thought).

Once when Sandra and some of us were sitting in the garden, Michelangelo who was doing some manual work in the garden came along and showed his mother how dusty his jumper was and how it had been made dirty by the work. I thought that was a clue to what the problem was. Michelangelo was still a child in a way, he hadn't really matured at all. One spoke to Stephan and one could see that there was a whole person there and very clear headed too.

Stephan gave the impression that he was attentive and intelligent. He had health issues because of all the drinking and unhealthy drug taking. He had survived all of it and spiritually he was a better person for having gone through those experiments. He spoke of it light heartedly as if it wasn't his own experience. He had read about the various drugs and tried them out on himself. He did whatever he did with open eyes and a mature responsible mind.

Equilibrium - Oil on canvas 1988

Michelangelo however reminded me of the noble red Indians who were given alcohol in order to make them drunk and keep them from doing better things.

Here and Now
Acrylic on canvas 1988

I had heard that drugs were given to young people nowadays to stop them from making too many demands on the controlling forces in society. He was really a small child in comparison to Stephan, even though they were both 35. Michelangelo sometimes came to dinner all dopey and it broke everyone's heart to see him that way. He would sit next to Stephan and his head would hover down on the food, he looked as if he was going to put his head down on the table for a long snooze. It was at one of these dinners that Lucilla came to say some bold things about relationships at the table. She said that Sandra seemed to prefer Stephan to her own son and treated him in a privileged manner. Sandra was sitting there with Michelangelo and Stephan sitting next to her, it was such a strong statement to make. Silence took over the dinner table it was almost a criticism that shook everyone out of their relaxed state of mind. Off came all their bourgeois niceties and high flying dinner talk, Lucilla was saying let's get real!

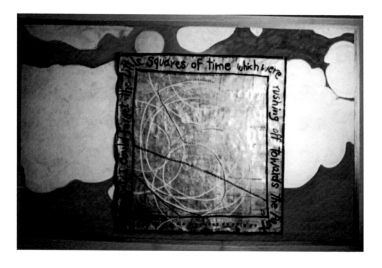

Dreamtime
Mixed media 1989

I was wondering what Lucilla expected from an overworked and disappointed mother. I mean how much could she ever support Michelangelo without ever getting any signs of improvement from him? Michelangelo of course didn't say anything. I really didn't realise the depth of this statement until someone shouted at Lucilla that she should shut up and get back to the kitchen where she belonged and that she had no right to say such things.

Stephan didn't say anything to defend himself, but Sandra was upset and so was everyone else and everyone started to shout and get angry at each other but mainly at Lucilla. Some defended her saying that she was only saying the truth and others disliked her for being disrespectful to Sandra at her own table. Some tried to calm people down. When everyone started to get back to normal, Lucilla was still trying to explain her point of view but saying that she was sorry how she put things and she was sorry about hurting anyone's feelings.

Dialogue No. 2
Watercolour 1986

I had seen with my friend Marina, that female's loyalties of people in the south of Italy always supported the men of the family at all costs. Marina would defend (her then boyfriend) totally and irrationally. I suppose that Lucilla had expected total loyalty from Sandra. However people in Tuscany aren't so family orientated as people in the south, I think their loyalties are for what they call "to reason" i.e. ragionare. It is very clear that Sandra was a social individual who didn't want to have to answer for her son who hadn't turned out as she had expected, and at times all her frustrations were poured out on him. There was no one strong enough to give her a helping hand in those moments of weakness.

People in the city
Pen and Ink

Later on after Christmas she found Maria Angelica a young Chilean woman who she had met at church. Maria Angelica was a beautiful girl with long auburn hair and a good figure, she was also a very good-hearted Christian friend. Maria Angelica started to give Sandra all the friendship she needed to keep Michelangelo and Stephan out of trouble. The question is why hadn't God sent her this angel before.

The Musicians
Oil on canvas 2008

After this dinner of contention Michelangelo wasn't feeling too good about Stephan because, Lucilla had voiced the thought which was a seed, an idea which hadn't occurred to him before. Michelangelo knew that Stephan was more sophisticated, but he was confident of his mother's love especially since she declared that she loved him in front of everybody. Michelangelo being a heart person was deeply aware in a quiet way, he wasn't stupid, he was only unable to express himself properly. Or was it because of all the pressure that he felt and all the demands made on him that he couldn't cope?

It was in the month before Christmas when Sandra asked me to stay with Michelangelo in her apartment in piazza ciompi as his assistant nurse.

I was to keep an eye on him through Christmas and the New Year. It was then that I got to know him a bit more and he told me what had happened to him as a young teenager. He said that he had been approached by some people when he was 16/17 and he felt that he could be powerful by hanging out with them. These people sold drugs. He tried to do everything in order to get out of it ever since, but that he suffered a lot and that at 35 he didn't want to suffer anymore.

It was strange that I had seen this person in a different light the first time I set eyes on him sitting on the sofa talking to Louise. He revealed himself to have a bundle of problems like everyone else. But, nevertheless he was a good person. I felt that he had been misunderstood many times and hadn't had the medicine that he had really needed. Sometimes God can send you down exactly what you need and that is what can be achieved if he has accepted your prayers. But Michelangelo hadn't believed in God that much.

It was getting close to Christmas. The day I arrived in Piazza dei Ciompi, I saw that Michelangelo could only use one hand. Nevertheless, he had wanted to do the cooking for the both of us.

After the meal he disappeared and when Sandra asked me where he was I said he hadn't come back. She told me to go upstairs and check if he was there (it was as if she knew what would happen). In fact he had gone upstairs with a bottle of wine and had drunk himself to sleep, poor thing, he must have felt very much alone. The next days as I got to know him better I found out that he didn't intend to spend Christmas with his family and wanted to spend it on his own in Florence. His feelings were well intact and it was surprising to find that he was very oriental in a way that only Asians can understand.

Piazzale Michelangelo
Watercolour 1999

Michelangelo didn't like Viareggio at all. It was because they had given him a hard time and he was very law abiding (very adherent and aware of the law). Compared to him I was an anarchist who feared nothing more than having no money in my pocket.

I had always liked Viareggio. As a student Patrizia had bought me to a pizza place right by the seaside and we had stuffed ourselves with pizza together with a bunch of rowdy teenagers. They were on the way home from school. It seemed like the authentic Italian Viareggio life, I mean people lived this life every day, having pizza before going back home.

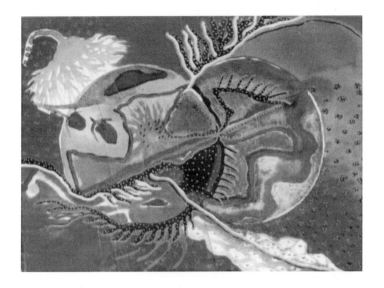

Without a title
Watercolour 1986

San Miniato
Watercolour 2002

We celebrated the Christmas of 2005 at Viareggio in the white villa. When Christmas day came the table was prepared at the big dining halls where I had seen the dinner laid that first night. It was a lovely do even similar to the lunches and dinners that my family have always prepared for relatives and friends in Pakistan and Iran. Prepared with a lot of love and affection.

Everyone got on well and Michelangelo and Stephan were well behaved and good. Michelangelo's Uncle Frederico proved to be very jovial and sociable, he was sort of Irish looking with reddish hair and beard and wanted everybody to feel at ease.

City View
Watercolour Collage 2002

His wife was a blond laptop owning lady who was looking at the business side of running their hotel and she was always busy with the emails.

One of their daughters had married a paraplegic, who was very intelligent and very up to date, but he couldn't move at all, his wife was a beautiful girl. One wondered about these young marriages, the other daughter was expecting with her husband they were both well settled in their life.

One thing that Frederico had said stuck in my mind even today, he said, "my mother in law irons my shirts for me and I am very grateful to her for this bit of affection". It seemed that she had won him over by doing that chore for him. As a young man Frederico had been to Iran and hadn't met any girls there and thought that it was very strange. I thought it was strange too, because he must have been there during the Shah's time when women were more westernised.

Dialogue No.3 – Watercolour

He was disappointed about this, but I wanted to tell him that Iranians as a people, are very reserved, especially the women and not very adventurous in their friendships even though they like foreigners and they usually want to practise their English – especially young people. However, men approaching women in Iran is not the done thing.

Even though in the new post-revolutionary age, it is surprising to see that women are more outgoing and would approach foreigners just to chat to them.

Visiting The Cathedral – Print Watercolour

I felt very ill at ease that Christmas, because I wasn't really supposed to be there.

But due to the fact that I had no money, I had ended up in this situation. Had I had my independence I would have probably spent Xmas and new year on my own as I had done in the past. But Sandra had a way of making an occasion of this Christmas. She put her old 60s vinyl's on an old gramophone and that's when she announced that she loved her son very much. She said that while we were sitting around the table and everyone was much surprised. It was like a gift for Michelangelo, after months of tension.

It was good that she did tell him that she loved him dearly, I mean it's always good for people to reveal their good feelings for each other as much as possible (instead of saying hurtful things). One never knows what happens the next day in life.

In fact, Michelangelo didn't survive the coming year, he passed away in his own bed in the beginning of March, he fell off the bed and went into a coma while everybody was sitting around him and passed away a month after that. Sometimes people recover from a coma but he didn't.

View From The Kitchen – Watercolour 2002

I don't know why Sandra's house and life reminded me so much of my mother's second cousins in Karachi.

I had seen that family live together in this big house and it seemed similar to how Italians live when they live together. They have their fights and there misunderstandings but they go on living together nevertheless. That is why people in the Middle East believe that some Italians have Eastern characteristics (because they are sociable and like to eat together). In Italy, eating in company is really important to people and sometimes, eating alone is looked upon as unpleasant.

Indian and Pakistani weddings and that sense of the family coming together, has a similar attitude of bringing everybody together for a joyful event. Even though things are changing now even in parts of Asia, some people don't have that much time for each other.

After the new year lunch and dinner Stephan started to study for his exams in order to get a degree and Sandra used to help him with his studies. I saw less of Lucilla because she worked in a restaurant in Pietra Santa and as a companion of an elderly lady.

Casa a Ventimiglia
Water colour

Once we were all down at the apartment in Florence in Piazza di Chompi and Louise Michelangelo's American friend was there too. That was when she was accused by one of the girls of having taken a shirt from the luggage. It was such an absurd accusation and I was sure that it was done in order to create unnecessary tension. I just couldn't believe this girl to be so mean. It was as if every once in a while some unpleasant thing had to be created on purpose in order to sweep away all the good feelings of friendship. I saw that happening often in other situations and other countries as well. At this point I defended Louise, because I respected her and thought of her highly. She was an amazingly informed and educated African American woman.

Dialogue No.4 (The Enigma) Watercolour 1990

She knew about things, which weren't about America and were about the rest of the world probably because she had gone to university in Russia. And she wasn't even Jewish! She reminded me of Condolisa Rice the woman who was Mr Bush Junior right hand woman in government at the time.

Ms Rice's speaking fluent Russian made me think that there were people who had followed in her footsteps and Louise was probably one of them. I will always remember the story of how Ms Rice had stood in the doorway to a merry Mr Yelstin who had had a glass too many (as far as I remember the anecdote I had read in the newspaper) she had spoken to him in Russian! I thought that was very impressive.

The Uffizzi Watercolour 2002

Sometimes Lucilla was very busy and she couldn't sit with old Mrs Pandini Sandra's mother, she would ask me to sit with her and I would do that on Sundays.

Sandra's mother was very fond of Sandra and always said that she would defend her daughter whole-heartedly and wouldn't allow anyone to speak badly of her.

She had been a young girl in the late 1800's when women use to wear big hats with flowers on them, and long romantic skirts with frilly starched tops. The type of thing that you see in films but she had pictures of herself with other girls dressed that way and she said that they were people that worked at their lace and embroidery producing factory.

Her parents who were Florentines had been pretty wealthy because of the factory; I loved to listen to the stories of how it used to be and how she had met her husband and how she had married. But more than anything I'll remember her for what she said after each meal, "Anche oggi si e mangiato"! which intends to say, "even today we have eaten a meal". Having lived through the war, I think she appreciated the fact that not everyone can procure the satisfying and tasty meals of the day and that is why one should be grateful for having the good wholesome meals served to us every day.

Without a title, Watercolour, 1987

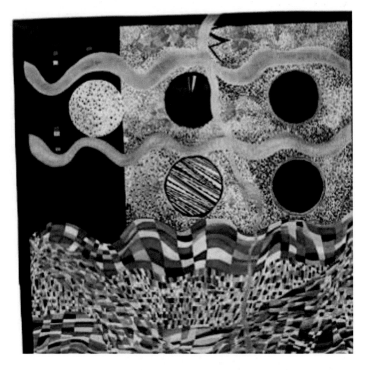

The Painting Ekstasis:

This picture came to represent my seeing the world in its smaller components; how everything is always organically and precisely mixing and mingling and changing from one thing to another in nature according to a plan.

This is a water picture, one about the two seas not mixing together.

It was Nadia who told me about the Koranic verse that and says that the sea waters are salty and fresh, but that they never mix with the currents of the freshwater that run in to the seas as if they were rivers running on land. Thanks to the mastermind who has had these systems run the world since time immemorial.

AL RAHMAN, Chap 55, v.19, 20.

"He sent the two waters that meet each other and between them there is a barrier which is not contaminated by fresh nor salt water, pearls and coral are extracted from both waters."

Al Rahman is the name of a chapter of the sacred Koran and means 'The Benevolent Creator'. It is a chapter which speaks about all of God's creations and the extraordinary things and the phenomena we find in nature; it asks the reader 'which one of these things can you negate?'

Had heard about the rivers flowing in the seas in some of the Jacques Cousteau films about the earth's waters. The concept of having rivers flowing in the oceans waters is still mind boggling. In this chapter in the sacred book in talks about the salty and the sweet waters which can never mix even when they are existing side by side in the seas and the oceans.

J'allais me donner picture

I like this painting very much, because of the balance I find it in. It is just right.

I was friends with Francesca and I think that's where I got the poem from – J'allais me donner. One day, I was at her house and she started reading T.S. Eliot's poem for me, 'The Love Song of J. Alfred Prufrock', which starts with:

Let us go then you and I
When the evening is spread out against the sky…

It has this tired air of dragging one's drunken feet on the pavement, and then every once and a while it says:

In the room the women come and go, talking of Michelangelo.

Eliot's poem is so much of our experience, I mean me and Francesca's. We had a feeling for the literature we were studying, especially Francesca who was truly a creative person. I found this poem in some book belonging to Francesca; she was giving me her deep feelings for Eliot's poems by reading out the love song poem to me.

It was such a gift of togetherness, but like all love and all good things, one knows that the apex is reached and then, one has to get back to reality. That's what 'J'allais me donner' means for me, especially concerning love. Worldly love and attachments are destined to fly away, as William Blake's poem says:

'He who kisses the joy as it flies
lives in eternity's sunrise'

'J'allais me donner' is the poem that was fitting to write on this image. It was even the expression of my feelings for Philippe, meaning that I had to let it go. He was never going to be mine and I was never allowed to be by his side, even as a friend.

However, God did allow me to have a cat named Mooshie and to whom I use to give all my love, because she was always there and tolerated my ups and downs, a true friend who was always there for me. The only thing she couldn't do was to provide me with groceries – and, I suppose, children. But even this little beloved creature was not mine, and one day we would have to part.

The poem 'J'allais me donner' was a prophecy about the future. Now in 2009, the fascists are in our lives, controlling our human relationships, and we have to pay ransom for everything, except for the breath we take, and this is what the poem was about;

'I was going to tell you that I loved you
but I realised that I didn't belong to myself'

Which is exactly what has happened ever since the year 2000 or thereabouts. Possibly, it was with breaking down of the Berlin wall that this Stasi type of control has overtaken the world. This system of hate goes directly against the Judeo-Christian idea of love and fraternity, and it considers money as the only God that we have to answer to. Therefore it creates deep ditches around the individuals who don't obey its orders. My brother, before his death, told me that he felt as if he had been thrown into a deep well and couldn't get out of it, his voice weak, as if he were really at the bottom of the well. Psychological pressures on him and other people.

'Il Flusso Organico', 1990

'The Organic Flow'

I was thinking of 'Ophelia', the picture painted by a Pre-Raphaelite painter.

I really love the romanticism of the character of Ophelia. However, Ophelia was a person who didn't fight in order to win. She wasn't thought to fight for things. She was a receiver, as most women are taught to be. Sometimes, I think that is a middle class attitude. You complacently wait for things to be given to you. But really speaking, Ophelia wasn't intelligent enough or experienced in the ways of life – she didn't even have a good friend to help her out. On top of it, she had a father who was a prohibiting moralist and was a negative influence in her life. As a woman, Ophelia wasn't a fortunate woman. Sometimes in the difficult project of 'husband chasing', girls get lucky and have the assistance they need from their mother, an elder sister or a friendly soul. One can't help thinking that had Ophelia known how to humour Hamlet, she might have saved him as well as her father and brother. She could have saved everybody had she been a 'bad' girl. As a more experienced and cunning and materialistic woman would have grabbed Hamlet the prince as a prize and she wouldn't have allowed him to get lost in his fantasises of revenge. How useless and negative Hamlet is as a personality. He takes the life of many innocent people and cultivates hate. So it is hate upon hate that we see on the stage. He tries to put things right and says that things shouldn't have happened the way they did. But really speaking, his interfering only brings darkness. I suppose what Shakespeare was really saying was that one bad deed brings with it a trail of other bad deeds. Opposite to this, we can see that one intelligent capable person who can save the peace at all costs may bring better times for himself and others around him. The organic flow is life itself – trickling and flowing water always finds a way. It is invincible and has no need for principles… It is a law unto its own. The laws which are inherent in nature, even if nature isn't kind, it automatically does what is supposed to do, showed a pretty girl who had drowned herself having suffered a broken heart. My painting is the before and the after scene. Ophelia disappears – only the flowing of the river remains and the plants that grow.

It is important that individuals are able to overcome the difficult moments of life and continue living the best life they can. It is the message that we get from Shakespeare; having the strength to continue even if life is getting us down, is the best policy and while we are trying to live our best life, helping others to live their lives as well as they can.

Having a correct attitude – the attitude of water which is life giving in its mere existence.

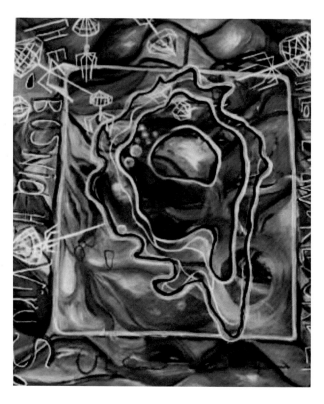

Virus Invading Bacteria,
Wednesday 28th October 2009

The viruses and the bacteria is a painting which was inspired by my studies of biology in London in 1980.

I was very impressed with the way the virus could inject their DNA into the body of a bacteria. In order to reproduce itself, a virus would use the body of the bacteria as a resource and in a short while, its DNA would turn into many. Then lots of little viruses would burst out of the empty shell of the bacteria. What would remain of the bacteria would be only the shell. Today I realise that the Maoist policy probably derives from scientific research. It seems that 'The Entity' will manage to take over the world by simply following what the virus does to the bacteria.

Is there anyone to study these political events in the light of this theory?

I feel it upon my life, and even though the invasion is being carried out very subtly and seemingly effortlessly in the Middle East, the fact that The Entity would never allow a Manfazar Alzeid – the Iraqi, who threw his shoes at President Bush – type to survive his freedom of speech and become a hero. That is what makes me fear this silent takeover by 'The Stasi Entity'. Some call it the Mongols conquering the rest of the world a second time around. But on the other hand, the wars of the white imperialists in the region are bitter and relentless. A war for resources has brought the West & its allies into lands whose people and mentality is well known to the Chinese who are Asians and are rather liked and respected by other populations of Asia. How can they ever be kept out of the race for resources by the ex-colonial powers who have also played the part of white racists who looked down at the people they conquered?

Poems

A Page From A Diary
21st OCTOBER 2003?

The linden trees on Independence Day
Fascinated dreamers
They cast a spell (with their giddy perfume)
You have to struggle to resist their magnetic force
Their temptation
Sprinkled mercilessly in the atmosphere
I am the only one who understands them
Perhaps because I am alone
This array of trees
They are
Unscrupulous and base
Predators
Who want to bend our will to their wishes
They want to make us give up resisting them
Their accomplice; cropped grass
Has a fresh perfume
Seemingly innocent
Together they are trying to…make me become like them
But they can't make me
You poor deceitful trees
Standing tall and ambitious
With your branches tensely reaching out
Out-towards the limits of the sky
Are you trying to hide-your fears?

The linden trees on Independence Day
I try to escape them

I struggle
In order to resist their temptation
Their magnetic force
Is in the giddy perfume
They sprinkle mercilessly in the atmosphere
The army of trees
They are
Cleverer than me
Unscrupulous and base
Predators
Who want us to bend to their wishes and whims
Who want to
Make us give up
Resisting them
The cropped grass
Is their accomplice
Together they are trying to make me become like them

You poor deceitful trees standing there
With your branches
Tensely reaching out
Towards the limits of the sky
Are you trying to hide
Your fears
You even recite poetry
Saying that you enjoy graceful occupations
Claiming for yourselves
Quiet greatness and noble simplicity…..
You make me pity you
Can you tell
Like primitive warriors and hunters
You are pulsating predators prowling
Looking out for fresh flesh
So that you can suck vitality and life
And turn into stone a creature who was roaming free
Even so, you claim to be graceful
Reciting the poetry, of
Quiet greatness and noble simplicity
You make me pity you
I can see you are like

Primitive warriors, or
Hunting predators
Prowling
You search for fresh flesh
So as to suck vitality and life
And turn into stone a creature who was roaming
I saw you and you were not in your usual sombre files
Seemingly old and static
Standing-solid
I observed you from a hidden place
While you began to dance
A dance of servile devotion, as if

You were dancing in a humble, servile fashion
Desiring to please
A severe judge –
You were dancing trees
Who bore coloured fiery flowers
Born out of the tension of the test
Which made you sprinkle
Your perfume in the air
While you pretended to be
Quiet and simple seemingly noble creatures

You were adoring a presence
Your trunks
Ridiculously rigid
When moving in the rhythm
You were trying to please
An invisible being
You were in prayer
To a divinity unknown
I saw you…
Whilst you held up above you, your thousand branches
Wantonly moving with the wind in
Voluptuously undulating movements
From root to each and every leaf-dancing in silent reverence

You were dancing in a humble, servile fashion
Desiring to please

A severe judge –
You were dancing trees
Who bore coloured fiery flowers
Born out of the tension of the test
Which made you sprinkle
Your perfume in the air
While you pretended to be
Quiet and simple seemingly noble creatures

I saw you and you were not in your usual sombre files
Seemingly cold and static
Standing tall and solid, placed on the ground.
I observed you from a hidden place,
While you danced
A dance of servile devotion, as if
You were adoring a pagan god
With rhythmical movements
Of your trunks
So ridiculously rigid
You were trying to please
An invisible being…..
A divinity
You were in prayer
To a being……..unknown
I saw you, did you know?
I saw you whilst with your thousands of branches
Held up above you harmoniously
With the wind blowing in undulating motion
Moving
Your bodies were from their
Roots to each and every leaf, in silent reverence

You were dancing in a humbly, servile fashion
Desiring to please
A severe presence (who judged you)
You were dancing trees
Who bore fiery flowers
The tension of the test

Made you sprinkle your perfume in the air
While you pretended
To be quiet and simple, even noble creatures

You were dancing in a humble, servile fashion
Desiring to please
A severe judge –
You were dancing trees
Who bore coloured fiery flowers
Born out of the tension of the test
Which made you sprinkle
Your perfume in the air
While you pretended to be
Quiet and simple seemingly noble creatures?

I am fascinated by you
Trees in love
But I try to escape from your spell

Song For Big Brother
Living In Big Brothers Surveillance Society

In the Temple of Profit, BB speaks to the congregation:
"If You Stick Out Your Tongue"
Maybe I won't hurt you
Cause by doing this
You are admitting submission
To the powers that be
You are adhering
To my point of view

The way I see things
You have got to play the game
According to my rules:
Weaknesses
Vulnerabilities, and your problems
Are good for my purpose
And when you are down
I am there beside You
To make use of the situation.

Each and every one of us
Thinks… Quite naturally
Live and let die…
Cause we have only got one life to live
And none of us wants to be caught by "the Bad Ass Roman
Emperor"
(He is not a nice person at all)
(He used to watch with pleasure the Christians thrown to the
animals)
So we say:
"Why not adhere"?

And each individual
Will do exactly as they are told
We all have a lot of things
We would like to achieve
A lot that we´d like to hold onto
Some people adhere
Because they live at the bottom of the social ladder
They like the power: Women
Women love having power
They love the power of putting the fear

The fear of god in you
"god" can take away your loved ones
God can reprimand you when you are having sex

Little "gods" are in all the nooks and crannies of your life
Streets full of CCTV´s
Rooms full of microphones
In Your homes and offices
Just so that we can control You
Big Brother is Here!

This is the way the decadent century begins
Say Goodbye to the free-world as you knew it
Security and Surveillance
Are here to stay
You might as well get used to it
Privacy is a luxury
The future is full of
Information manipulators (who put microchips where ever they
please)
Microphones and CCTV´s
Will cover our cities and our lives
Spies and stalkers in the streets
Listening to every word
Reporting moves and political opinions
(Doesn´t it remind you of North Korea ?)
(Or military rule in Burma?)

People in many countries have lived,
With Big Brother watching them for many years
Why should You be Free?
Why should you live a spontaneous life?
Where love and anger and other emotions
Were not speculated upon
Now that we have gotten a TV
Watching every bodies life
Like little gods behind the scene
We sit:
Omniscient and omnipotent....

If You stick out your tongue
I promise I won´t hurt you
If you are one of "Us"
We will make sure that you are well connected
We will look after you;
See to it that you get things done (you get more information)
Carry out my orders
And I will give you the right instructions
In order to get on in the competition
I can read your innermost thoughts and fears
So Fear and Love
Your beloved protector and benefactor.
Be loyal to me
So that my voice shall be your voice
And I will allow you to use your PC
I will allow you to get on with your life.

"You must stick out your tongue"
You must reassure me
That You belong to Me,
You are saying that the cultural differences between us don´t exist
You are assuring me that you fear
The "Islamic Bogymen"
That You are not a nuisance
 Or a dangerous minded person.
That you will not dare to "believe "in anything else.

Stick out your tongue (at the corner of your mouth)
And I will give you Joy,
Joy in Business and material gain.

The people say under their breath:
Oh Big Brother!
I know which way my bread is buttered
Please don´t mess up my life
You exercise pure Power
I know you are here to stay!
Cause you are protecting us

By milk shaking our brains
Rightly you are creating
Homogenized… Zombies

Big Brother says:
I want to create a New World Order
Where feelings of humanity are banished for ever,
My Religion is based on Profit,
You have to realize, that nothing is for free
Not even the breath you are taking.
You have to pay for
All the benefits you are receiving.
Like Abraham's God
We want to rule your hearts and minds
(Abraham broke the Idols in the Temple if you remember)

"Stick out your tongue"
And I promise I won´t hurt you
Or your beloved ones
And the benefits are
That you will be connected
And perhaps
I will allow you to live
A little.

(I am taken aback by the self confidence
And yet I dream

That one day
The situation will turn around
And I won´t have to be eating humble pie
One day soon the wheel of fortune will do justice
And I hope that I will have the last laugh
There have always been unjust big brothers in the world
They think they can get away
With all the sufferance they cause
I hope that God who has created the universe
Will finally look at us
And make Big Brother Back Off
Cause we just want to live in peace
And love our neighbour as much as one of us…
The persecutions and the Inquisitions
Did manage to succeed
But why do we always have to go back to those things?
Mr B a famous politician says he has chosen this policy
Of "the survival of the fittest"
Because he wants to save
"Our way of life"
But meanwhile he gets paid for giving talks
About how he would solve the questions on the table
And then he politely bows out
Having contributed nothing at all
And yet we idiots believed in him.)

May 2012

I started writing this poem when I was in Tehran, in 2006. I had come away from Viareggio and had started to live with my brother and my mother again in 2006.

I had had an Art Studio in via Fiesolana from 1998 to 2004 and had experienced a lot of pressure from anonymous people who used to get in and out of my studio when I was not in it myself. They used to take things which were important to me. And afterwards someone would appear and stare at me hard. This always frightened the life out of me. Once a young girl came in and she had such an omnipotent expression on her face while she was staring... It was very strange, and I wish I could have asked her, "what do you want?".

But I had no strength to protect myself from such hard hearted gazes.

Another time a smiling girl came, and I will always be grateful for her smile. A lot of inexplicable things were going on. One day at the bank I saw a non-Italian white woman approaching the bank manager all tongue, she was rolling it out so much ... in front of everybody watching her .... And I thought "what is going on here?"

One of my friends said that it meant "do you want to have sex?" The married women I knew were all into it. In my mind I was really confused. If I had had a TV I would have probably caught onto what was going on.... But I had not watched TV for ten years and I had painted and read books and prayed. It seemed too diffuse and common when I was out in the world again in 1998.

I was pondering the meaning for many years, even in Tehran it was the biggest trend. So much so that you seemed to not get anything done without doing it.

That's why I thought about putting my feelings of fear and my suffering from not having adhered to it in words.

I will never forget all the harm I received by this "religious" group. Their persecution will probably never leave their victims alone.

This is the poem "pages from a diary" in Italian
I have written them in this language to begin with and then
translated them into English.

Pagina Dal Diario

"Canzone agli Alberi della piazza d´Indipendenza"

Subisco il fascino

Ma cerco di fuggire l´incanto
Ogni giorno cerco di resistere alla tentazione
Ogni mattina lotto contro la forza magnetica;
Il profumo inebriante ´degli alberi e´ sparso impiestosamente nell
aria
E´ un gioca difficile
Io sono sola di fronte all'esercito degli alberi
Loro sono pin furbi di me;
"Ignobilmente senza scrupoli"
Vogliono assoggettarrni alla loro volonta'
Cercano di rompere la mia resistenza
E hanno la complicita'
E l'amicizia dell'erba appena tagliata
Alberi; poveri paralizzati creature…..
Sempre con le vostre mani estese in tensione
Verso il limite dell'atmosfera
Mascherate la vostra vita interiore con
"Stille grosse und edle einfalt"
con la tranquilla grandezza e nobile semplicita',
mi fate pena sapete?
Mi fate pena perche come gli antichi cacciatori,
oppure gli uomini primitivi
Cercate la viva carne fresca e pulsante
Una preda cercate
Per sbranarlo e succhiare la linfa vitale di quella
Che prima esisteva in libero movimento

Una mattina mentre passavo dalla piazza
Vi ho visto e non eravate pin eretti e fermi come sempre
Di nascosto, vi osservavo dall'angoli degli occhi, mentre
Voi in un balletto devoto e servile
Come gli adoratori pagani
Con movimenti ritmici di vostri tronchi rigidamente
ridicoli
Cercavate di compiacere
A un essere divino ed invisibile
Voi alberi freddi e marmorei
Adoravate un essere
Frantumato…..sapete?
Vi ho visto…..sapete?
Vi ho visto che con le mille mani
In estensione verso l'infinito
Con le vostre braccia
E movimenti
Armoniosamente ondulanti
Pulsavate dalle radici sino
Alle estremita' delle foglie…..
Di una volutta' soffocata
Eravate servilmente umili e ardentemente
Deridersosi di compiacere ad un essere divino

Un severo gindice per il quale danzavate

Danzarate o alberi e ogni mattina,
Dalla tensione della prova
Vi nascevano dei Fiori di fuoco che spargevano
Impietosamente il vostro profumo
"Stille grobe und edle einfalt"
Subisco il fascino di voi alberi in amore,
Ma cerco di fuggire l'incanto…

11th February 1993

Out There

Out There, Out There
So many people are doing their own thing,
Walking, Talking, Working, Calculating
And the Cash Register
Is always Ringing.
Money is lost,
And Money is gained
That is the eternal story
Of The People walking to and fro,
They are used and abused
They do use and abuse,
Out There, out There.
Here
I live in a picture of my own
I Do and Do and Do Dream
Here am I
I am sitting Here
Dreaming of the wide Horizons of Possibility
Dreaming like youth of what is to come
Dreaming of the wide Horizons of Probability
There are so many people Out There
Who think in a logical rational way
They Walk , Talk, Work, Calculate
They
They are changing the world
Money is lost
And Money is gained
In Factories and Chemical Industries
The new science religion of Nuclear Power and Energy
Sends Spaceships to Mars and Mercury
That, is the Eternal Story
Of Destruction, and Construction
Out There, Out There.

Here,
Here I Sit in a picture of my own
I Do Dream
And my hands are tied behind my back
Here I sit thinking of the friends that I don't make
Of the good Music in me that no one hears
Yes!
They are changing the face of this earth
And I am embarrassed.
Here I sit in a picture of my own
Dreaming of the wide Horizons of Possibility
Dreaming like youth of what is to come
Dreaming of the wide Horizons of Probability.
And Hope still lives in me
Now;
Now is the Time
For my Dreams to step out
It is Time Now
For the paintings which live in my imagination
For the children who live in the center of my cells
For the Music which plays my sentiments so clear
And for the Poetry which wills to have its own way
It is Time now for them to step out
And give me a Face; a Place; an Identity
In the reality
Out There.
Out There,
People Do Dream, and Dream, and Dream
They Listen intently at the throbbing of their hearts
They Sit and Register on their Souls center,
They register like Seismographs
The reality.
Here
We Sit
Looking out of the Windows of our Homes
We Sit Here
Dreaming
Dreaming

Dreaming about the wide Horizons of Possibility
Dreaming like Youth of what is to come,
Dreaming of the wide Horizons of Probability.
Oh rational self,
You always want to control life
with your Horizontal and Vertical lines,
Lines which go up and down,
left and right,
So that you can protect yourself from suffering
In the immense Sea
Of the irrational.
The irrational life which throws you here and there and
everywhere.

This poem is an 'animation' short film produced by me on YouTube.